Marxism and the English Revolution

John Rees

WHALEBONE
PRESS

The truth is the whole. The whole, however, is merely the essential nature reaching its completeness through the process of its own development.

G. W. F. Hegel, *The Phenomenology of Spirit*, 1807

The writing of history has always been a battle against the self-styled expert … Modesty, judgement, imagination, a sensitivity to connections: these are what all historians need over and above the special techniques of their particular sub-disciplines … The attempt to see connections is hazardous and may lead to mistakes. But these can be corrected. Failure to look for connections leads to barrenness, myopia, blinkers.

Christopher Hill, *Partial Historians and Total History*, 1972

The whole is not the sum of the parts. The parts find their meaning only in their relationship to the whole, in their integration into the totality. The category of the totality, however, does not in any way suppress the individual moments. It is not an undifferentiated unity in which concrete phenomena disappear.

Franz Jakubowski, *Ideology and Superstructure in Historical Materialism*, 1936

History does nothing, it 'possesses no immense wealth', it 'wages no battles'. It is man, real, living man who does all that, who possesses and fights; 'history' is not, as it were, a person apart, using man as a means to achieve its own aims; history is nothing but the activity of man pursuing his aims.

Karl Marx and Frederick Engels, *The Holy Family*, 1845

Marxism and the English Revolution

First published in Great Britain in 2024 by Whalebone Press,
c/o Counterfire, Busworks, 39 North Road, London N7 9DP.
Cover design: Ian Goodyear for Ranged Left Design
Layout: Neil Darby

ISBN 978-1-907899-17-1

A catalogue record for this book is available from the British Library.

Printed and bound in Great Britain.

Whalebone Press is an imprint of Counterfire
www.counterfire.org

Contents

About the author

John Rees is a writer, broadcaster, and activist. He is the author of seven major titles and his latest book, *The Leveller Revolution*, was published by Verso. His forthcoming major study of popular politics in the English Revolution, *The Fiery Spirits*, will also be published by Verso in early 2025. He is a Visiting Research Fellow at Goldsmiths, University of London, a co-founder of the Stop the War Coalition, and a spokesperson for the People's Assembly.

Abbreviations

BL:	British Library
CJ:	Journal of the House of Commons
CSPD:	Calendar of State Papers Domestic
CSPV:	Calendar of State Papers Venetian
LJ:	Journal of the House of Lords
HMC:	Historical Manuscripts Commission
MECW:	Marx-Engels Collected Works
ODNB:	Oxford Dictionary of National Biography
PRO or TNA:	Public Records Office, now The National Archive
STC:	Short Title Catalogue. A. Pollard and G. Redgrave, A Short Title Catalogue of Books Printed in England, Scotland and Ireland, and of English Books Printed Abroad 1475-1640.
STC (2nd edn.):	A Short Title Catalogue of Books Printed in England, Scotland and Ireland, and of English Books Printed Abroad 1475-1640, 2nd edition, revised and enlarged, begun by W. Jackson and F. Fergusson, completed by K. Pantzer.
Wing:	D. Wing, A Short Title Catalogue of Books Printed in England, Scotland, Ireland, Wales and British America and of English Books Printed in Other Countries, 1641-1700 (1945-51).

Introduction

The Marxist interpretation of the English Revolution, while never the dominant strand of thought among historians, was at least taken seriously enough to be influential until the late 1970s. At that point the then new wave of revisionist historians developed a critique of both Whig and Marxist explanations, often confused with each other, which denied that there were any long-term causes of the revolution or that there was any effective relationship between the class structure of society and the revolutionary upheaval of the 1640s. Methodologically this was justified as a critique of Marxism's supposed reductionism and teleology. This book is born of a desire to set the record straight. The record in question is that of the Marxist contribution to understanding of the English Revolution of the mid-seventeenth century. The need for such clarification arises from the current state of the debate about the revolution.

Revisionism was essentially a series of negatives: local, or multi-national, but not national; contingent and accidental, not necessary; short term and personal, not long term and structural; political and religious, not social and economic. Gradually, the virtues of negative critique, such as they were, became exhausted. They became exhausted because historians painstakingly proved what dialecticians know instinctively: that negative polarities are often overcome in an inclusive totality. Linguistically this can be achieved by replacing a negative 'not' with an inclusive 'and'. Local, multi-national *and* national; contingent *and* necessary; short term *and* structural; political, religious *and* socio-economic. But although methodology may help preserve us from error and may point us to productive ways of looking at the structure of society, alone it cannot do the heavy lifting of actually constructing a concrete account of historical development.

It is this challenge which now confronts historians. Revisionism is far behind us. Indeed, as Peter Lake and Jason Peacey's important survey of the current state of seventeenth-century studies argues, 'the "post-revisionist" reaction has been prolonged and powerful'. But, nevertheless, the evaporation of revisionism has been partial. The recovery of civil-war radicalism has been considerable. The destruction of the conservative framing of local or county studies has been extensive, notably in the work of Ann Hughes and Clive Holmes. Social history has often come to fill the vacuum created by revisionism's concentration on high politics. Lake and Peacey give an admirable account of this new work being done by historians, but it's less easy to agree with the contention that, 'Post-revisionism ... made much greater impact in dealing with the *causes* of the civil wars than with understanding its *course* and its *consequences*'. Tim Harris' contribution to the post-revisionist discussion, 'Revisiting the Causes of the English Civil War', is relatively rare in confronting the issue head-on. Lake and Peacey may see rather more in this discussion because of the agreement between late revisionism and post-revisionism about the importance of religion. But explanations based on religion only provide an essential but partial account of the causes of the revolution if they downplay the relationship between religion and wider socio-economic developments or, for that matter, the independent causation that originates in the socio-economic structure of society.[1]

This, in turn, perhaps stems from a concern, admirable in some ways, not to simply return to old debates. Lake and Peacey praise the post-revisionist desire to '*engage* with revisionist arguments rather than to "turn back the clock" by reviving the older grand narratives'. But, while the mere re-hashing of old discussions would certainly be tedious, it remains true that any progress involves a return to our past thoughts in new circumstances. Critique also means recovery. Older scholarship is not necessarily worse scholarship. In particular this book is concerned to rectify some misrepresentations of Marxism that remain from the revisionist era and to suggest that an area that still remains to be seriously revisited is the

[1] P. Lake and J. Peacey, 'Introduction: rethinking public politics in the English Revolution' in P. Lake and J. Peacey (eds.), *Insolent Proceedings, Rethinking public politics in the English Revolution* (Manchester, MUP, 2022), pp.1-2. T. Harris, 'Revisiting the Causes of the English Civil War', *Huntington Library Quarterly*, vol.78 no.4 (2015), pp.615-35.

role of socio-economic structures as effective causes of the English Revolution. The new social history in part moves in this direction, but it sometimes seems, in reaction to revisionism's concentration on high politics, to be dislocated from questions of political power. John Walter has recently argued that 'most social historians … inasmuch as they were aware of the debates Revisionism engendered, were happy to let the political historians slug it out' and that they 'pursued an agenda that compounded the distancing between social and political history.' Walters sees some convergence with post-revisionist political historians now, but admits 'much social history carried on as before, fragmenting into further specialization, taking its practitioners further away from dialogue with political historians, and no longer aspiring to an earlier ambition to produce a totalising history of society'.[2]

In arguing for a new synthesis, I hope to suggest that post-revisionism might lead to the emergence of a more positive school or schools of thought with an identifiable explanation of why the nations of these islands developed in the way they did in the seventeenth century. As it is, it appears that attempts to test new syntheses are still deterred by the long shadow of revisionism and its hostility to such projects.

This short book is not an attempt to scale that mountain. Its purpose is more modest. It is an attempt to address a certain imprecision and carelessness in discussing what Marxist analysis might have to offer the post-revisionist moment. Let me give a couple of examples. Glenn Burgess' much cited overview of revisionism argued that,

---

[2] P. Lake and J. Peacey, 'Introduction: rethinking public politics in the English Revolution' in P. Lake and J. Peacey (eds.), *Insolent Proceedings, Rethinking public politics in the English Revolution*, pp.2-3. J. Walter, 'Kissing Cousins? Social History/Political History before and after the Revisionist Moment', *Huntington Library Quarterly*, Vol.78, No.4 (Winter 2015), pp.703, 704, 721. Some similar points about social history are made by Mike Braddick and Phil Withington in their introduction to M. J. Braddick and P. Withington, *Popular Culture and Political Agency in Early Modern England and Ireland* (Woodbridge, Boydell, 2017), pp.1-15.

> The chief characteristic of the work done in the 1950s, 1960s and early 1970s (whether from the Marxist perspective of Hill or the sociological perspectives of Stone and Zagorin) was an attempt to graft onto a basically whig political history some sort of social dimension. The problem with this was not that no satisfactory or meaningful links could be made between society and politics. Rather, the links that could be made were coming to be seen as over-reliant on reductionist assumptions.[3]

There are serious problems with this statement. For instance, Marxist history is not a continuation or variant of Whig history but a root-and-branch critique of it. And, while not the subject of this book, Whig history is not primarily a reductionist framework. Its major fault is its teleology, for which Marxists have roundly criticised it. Burgess is careful not to claim that Stone was a Marxist. Others have been less careful, despite the fact that Stone was explicit that 'the class war theory of Marxists has only limited applicability to the seventeenth century' and went on to decry 'their persistent attempts to link these developments [the rise of capitalism] to the revolution by means of a theory of class warfare.' But these issues can be examined on another occasion. What concerns us here is that the charge of economic reductionism is routine and unexamined. Part of the difficulty with these discussions is that so few specific examples of supposed reductionist analysis are actually cited. Out of the 66 footnotes in Burgess' essay, Christopher Hill is cited three times and Brian Manning once, but never to demonstrate the central contention that Marxism is reductionist.[4]

---

[3] G. Burgess, 'On Revisionism: An Analysis of Early Stuart Historiography in the 1970s and 1980s', *The Historical Journal*, Vol. 33, No. 3 (Sep. 1990), p. 609.

[4] G. Burgess, 'On Revisionism: An Analysis of Early Stuart Historiography in the 1970s and 1980s', pp.609-27. L. Stone, 'The English Revolution' in R. Forster and J. P. Greene, *Preconditions of Revolution in Early Modern Europe* (Baltimore, John Hopkins Press, 1970), p.61. John Walter is right to say that Stone wrote 'under the umbrella of Weber, not Marx', see J. Walter, 'Kissing Cousins?', p.705. See also T. Harris, 'Revisiting the Causes of the English Civil War', pp.615-35.

Finally, in one of Sean Kelsey's recent investigations of whether the execution of Charles I in 1649 was pre-determined, he argues that the practitioners of 'Marxist historiography' believe that 'if the death of Charles I was the inescapable consequence of social and economic change, then the manner in which it came about was of little essential relevance'. We are never told who exactly are these Marxists. They are neither named in the text nor cited in any footnote.[5]

This book attempts to rectify some these misconceptions about what contemporary Marxists argue, and at revisiting the debates about whether and how class worked in the seventeenth century and its relationships with politics. It is aimed at demonstrating the relevance of Marxism to some of the questions that are going begging in the post-revisionist landscape.

Chapter 1 is designed to make a gesture in the direction of one of the areas that Lake and Peacey identify as in need of more study: 'There is so much that remains to be done on the wider geographical landscape of the civil wars, in terms of the relationship between events in England and in Continental Europe....' I hope at least to demonstrate that any comparative study of the English Revolution and other revolutionary uprisings in Europe in the 1640s inevitably raises the issue of the respective long-term causes and socio-economic contexts of these rebellions. The Leveller supporter and agitator Edward Sexby had the experience, like Tom Paine in the following century, of fighting in two revolutions, the English and the rising of the *Ormee* in Bordeaux. In both, he espoused the political positions of the Leveller's *Agreement of the People*, and indeed had that document translated into French. But the fate of those two Republican projects were dramatically different. Why? To understand the answer to this, the Edward Sexby question so-to-say, requires historians to return to the kind of discussion which was once common in the historiography of the period, but is now much less so: what were the differences in the long-term causes and in the class structures of the various European mid-century upheavals? A brief description of the risings in Bordeaux, Naples, Sicily, and Catalonia are used to examine this issue.

---

[5] S. Kelsey, 'The Trial of Charles I', *The English Historical Review*, Vol.118, No.477 (June 2003), p.583.

Chapter 2 is largely analytical and methodological in nature. It examines some widely held misunderstandings and simplifications of Marxist concepts as they apply to the English Revolution. The aim is to dispel the more misleading and misguided descriptions of Marxism and to suggest a more sophisticated model of social class and politics than is often assumed to exist in the work of Marx and in the work of contemporary Marxist historians of the seventeenth century. This defence of Marxist categories will not necessarily win over critics of Marxism, but it may at least result in a better informed, less dismissive, more fruitful argument.

Chapters 3 and 4 apply this approach to the class structure of England in the 1600s, in one case by looking at how the politics of the Levellers related both to the middling sort and to the labouring poor and, in the other case, by looking at the social profile of the middling sort. It is an essential part of this argument to address the objection to class analysis which rests on pointing out that not all of, say, the middling sort expressed themselves politically by support for a single political project. This really should not be either a surprise or an objection to the use of class categories in description of England in the seventeenth century. After all, it is a commonplace of contemporary politics that a single social class, for instance the modern working class, can support a number of rival political organisations, social democratic and communist for instance, not to mention the existence of working-class conservatism. Why would we not expect similar diverse political strategies to arise from perhaps less well-defined classes in the seventeenth century? Class analysis may be mistaken, but not because classes give rise to multiple political projects.

The final chapter provides an overview of historiographical debates about the Levellers, describing how both the findings of research and the political and social context within which historians wrote has shaped what we know about these revolutionaries. The chapter celebrates the recent revival of interest in the radicals of the 1640s, but its ultimate purpose is to turn the tools of Marxist analysis onto the writers of history themselves, describing not only what was written but outlining the influence of the context in which it was written.

I am grateful to Ariel Hessayon for discussion of some of these themes over the years and to Elaine Graham-Leigh, Waseem Ahmed, Dominic Alexander and Lindsey German for commenting on the draft. Some of these thoughts have been published before, but all the chapters have been revised for publication here. Chapter 3 originally appeared in *Bunyan Studies*, in Chapter 4 I have drawn on my initial review of Peter Earles' book for *International Socialism*, and Chapter 5 is based on work I did for my doctoral research that has not previously been published.[6]

[6] J. Rees, 'The Levellers, the Labouring Classes, and the Poor', *Bunyan Studies*, No. 24 (2020), pp.15-30. J. Rees, 'The rising bourgeoisie', *International Socialism*, No.46 (London, Spring 1990), pp.159-65.

Chapter 1

The Edward Sexby question

There is no doubt that Edward Sexby's life was in danger in his night-time escape over the mediaeval walls of seventeenth-century Bordeaux. Ascending and descending the three-storey-high battlements in the pitch black was a dangerous enough. But that was not the worst of it. Sexby was fleeing victorious royalists bent on executing the leaders of the republican movement that had taken power in the city. One of his compatriots, John Tubbing, had already been caught and 'stripped, robbed' and 'put in prison'. There he had been 'racked', and, as Sexby later reported, because 'he kept secret what he knew, the torture cost him his life'.

In Sexby's favour was the fact that this was not the first time he had risked his life in pursuit of a republican project. He had done so many times. Sexby had been an officer in Oliver Cromwell's Ironsides in 1643 and a trooper in Sir Thomas Fairfax's cavalry regiment after that, and likely saw action in some the most dramatic and deadly battles of the civil war. But it was not only on the battlefield that Sexby had been involved in possibly fatal actions. He had been one of the leading agitators of the mutiny in the New Model Army in 1647. It was a mutiny which, had it been unsuccessful, might well have ended with its leaders paying the ultimate price for their defiance of the moderate majority in the House of Commons. He had possibly been with Cornet Joyce when troopers from the New Model Army seized King Charles in 1647 and was one of the main supporters of the Levellers' *Agreement of the People* later the same year. Sexby was back on the field of battle the following year. He fought at the battle of Preston in 1648 and he was the trusted messenger who brought Cromwell's report of that victory to the Commons. He was already acting as intermediary between Leveller leader John Lilburne and Cromwell in the months that led to the trial and execution of the King. Sexby was still in his late thirties in 1653, the year of his escape from Bordeaux, and he had already had a career which historian Gerald Aylmer has described as 'one which only the most reckless historical novelist would dare to invent!'. But even by these standards, the presence of this former grocer's apprentice and experienced revolutionary in Bordeaux at the height of a second republican revolution requires some explanation.[1]

I

France, like England, was undergoing a social convulsion. In the years 1635-1660, Provence alone saw 156 popular revolts, Aquitaine even more at 282, an annual average of 6.3 and 11.3 respectively. The rebellion was called the Fronde, the word for the sling that that Parisian crowds used to smash the windows of their overlords. The emblem of the Fronde appeared on hats, gloves, women's fans, and was baked onto bread. The rebellion lasted from 1648 to 1653 and was reaching the climax of its last phase in Bordeaux where a republican movement was emerging. The French state was ruled by Anne of Austria, Spanish by birth and regent for the King still in his minority, and by her Cardinal, in origin a poor Sicilian named Guilio Mazarini, naturalised to Mazarin. The powerful 'princes of the blood', Orleans and Condé, were the most prominent but not the only court rivals for power. The Crown was profligate and indebted, a situation made extreme by a war with Spain begun in 1635. Taxation of all classes was ramped-up and sales of office were extended, much to the dislike of the existing beneficiaries. The government was widely unpopular, Mazarin especially so, as the flood of 5,000 scurrilous pamphlets targeting him testified. The Estates General

---

[1] E. Ludlow, *The Memoirs of Edmund Ludlow*, Vol. I (Oxford, Clarendon Press, 1894), p.415. *CSPD: Interregnum, 1654* (London, 1880), pp.139-94. *CSPD: Interregnum*, 1657-8 (London, 1884), pp.86-115. S. K. Roberts (ed.), *The Cromwell Association Online Directory of Parliamentarian Army Officers* (2017). H. N. Brailsford, *The Levellers and the English Revolution* (Nottingham, Spokesman, 1961), Ch.XXXV. D. F. Lawson, '"*Upon a Dangerous Design*", *The Career of Edward Sexby, 1647-1657*' (PhD. thesis, University of Alabama, 2016), pp.17, 159. G. Aylmer (ed.), *The Levellers and the English Revolution* (London, Thames and Hudson, 1975), p.24. Sexby is poorly served by his portrayal as a thoughtless firebrand by John Simm in the otherwise excellent TV series *The Devils Whore* (2008).

had not met since 1614 and would not do so until the Revolution of 1789. The only representative body to stand out against the Crown was the *Parlement de Paris*, not actually a parliament in the English sense but the highest court in the land with a semi-veto over Royal edicts. As discontent mounted, the *Parlement* forced on the Crown a series of reforms, some similar to measures taken by the Long Parliament.[2]

The government thought it had quietened the resistance enough to arrest the most prominent oppositionists. It was a bad miscalculation. On 27 August 1648, the Parisian masses took to the streets. Some 1,000 barricades blocked the streets of the capital and Anne of Austria and Mazarin were besieged in the Palais Royal. The Crown had to retreat and practically the whole of the *Parlement*'s demands were granted. The Fronde was victorious. But it was an uneasy peace that marked the end of the *Fronde Parlementaire*. Neither the Crown nor the opposition had managed to define a new order. Into this vacuum stepped the Fronde of the Princes. What gave the second Fronde its force was the revolt of the provinces, not pacified by the settlement in Paris. And even Paris was once again at boiling point when remarks by the regent, to the effect that the *Parlement* and bourgeois of Paris were all Cromwells and Fairfaxes who wanted to abolish the blood royal in France and establish a republic as in England, became known. But eventually the Crown regained the initiative, quelling the revolts in the provinces one by one. The last to hold out was the rebellion in Bordeaux. The Duke of Condé's involvement in the Bordeaux rebellion did nothing to strengthen it, and his alliance with Spain brought it no relief. It was, nevertheless, the most advanced point that the whole of the Fronde reached and its appeal to English republicans is understandable.[3]

The south-west of France had a long radical tradition dating back

---

[2] G. Parker, 'Crisis and Catastrophe: The Global Crisis of the Seventeenth Century Reconsidered', *The American Historical Review*, Vol.113, No.4 (Oct. 2008), Table 1, p.1056. R. B. Merriman, *Six Contemporaneous Revolutions* (Oxford, Clarendon Press, 1938), pp.53-5. Still a valuable account of the Fronde, proving that older scholarship is not necessarily worse scholarship.

[3] Merriman, *Six Contemporaneous Revolutions*, pp. 63-7.

to the Albigensians, the twelfth- and thirteenth-century heretical sect that was motivated in part by anticlericalism. In 1594, the revolt of *Les Croquants*, or Clodhoppers, as their feudal lords christened them, swept the region. In the seventeenth century, the masses rose again against eyewatering tax impositions which worsened the conditions inflicted by poor harvests and epidemics. 'The result was a permanent state of unrest', writes one historian of the Fronde, 'attacks on tax collectors' and 'isolated riots could easily lead to organised revolt', sometimes encouraged by nobles pursuing their own dynastic ambitions. Huguenot protestants formed a considerable minority in the region, accustomed to looking to the reformed religion of England for assistance, even if they had been abandoned by Charles I's regime at La Rochelle a generation earlier. Substantial trade with England, including perhaps a third of Bordeaux's wine exports, brought with it the influence of the revolution in England. The Venetian ambassador to France thought that 'the English going yearly to Bordeaux to ship wines has given them ample means not only of establishing many connections there, but ... of impressing their own opinions on the inhabitants.' There were republican sentiments preached in Bordeaux pulpits from at least 1650. The most consistent of those republicans were the *Ormee*, meaning elm tree, so named after the stand of elms in Bordeaux under which the radicals would meet. With a base among the same kind of middling sort of merchants and artisans as the London radicals, and organised in trade friendly societies, some could be heard announcing affinity with the Independents and *les Niveleurs*, or Levellers, from about this time. Republicans in Bordeaux seemed to have worn green ribbons, like the Levellers, as a sign of rebellion and were the first ever to raise the red flag as a symbol of revolt, flying it from the spire of St. Michael's church.[4]

English republicans were certainly following the Fronde, and events in Bordeaux in particular, with close interest. The gadfly journalist Marchamont Nedham was in charge of the widely read *Mer-*

---

[4] Mercurius Politicus (21-28 July 1653), p.2604. E. 708 [2]. H. N. Brailsford, *The Levellers and the English Revolution*, pp.674-5. R. Mousnier, 'The Fronde', in R. Forster and J. P. Greene, *Preconditions of Revolution in Early Modern Europe*, pp.136-7.

curius Politicus. This was a pro-government weekly and it reported on the cause of the rebels in Bordeaux regularly and sympathetically. *Politicus* saw in the Bordeaux revolt a protest against 'the sacred Trifle of Prerogative and Monarchy', and it encouraged the French to cast aside 'your old Vive Le Roy's, and let A liberte, Monsieur, be the new cry throughout all your Nation'. It denounced backsliders in the Bordeaux Parliament for resiling from their call to the people 'that now was the Time, or never, to shake off their Collars and Chaines, and stand for their Freedom.' It told its readers that 'None are so eminent for their activity and courage as the brave Bourdelois' and complimented them on behaving like 'brave Roundheads' in defying the 'Court Cavaliers'.[5]

The network of relationships into which Sexby had entered at the epicentre of the English Revolution now propelled him into the centre of events in Bordeaux. As well as Cromwell's trusted officer and an ally of Lilburne, Sexby had also become an associate of MP Henry Marten, the regicide and republican. When exactly Sexby and Marten first met is lost to us, but it was likely to have been in the later 1640s. In the political turmoil that attended the execution of the King in 1649, these influential figures in Sexby's life, so recently allies in opposing the King, had taken very different roads. Cromwell and Marten were members of the Council of State, the ruling body of the new Republic. Lilburne was unsuccessfully tried for treason and successfully exiled by the new regime for his demand that they should call new elections and not rely on the might of the army as the source of their power. Sexby's sympathies lay with Lilburne, but he stayed on in the army, promoted to Colonel, until he was cashiered after a dispute with the troops under his command.

---

[5] *Mercurius Politicus* (4-11 July 1650), p.76. E. 607 [12]. *Mercurius Politicus* (24 July-1 Aug. 1650), p.123. E. 608 [18]. *Mercurius Politicus* (15-22 Aug. 1650), p.151. E. 610 [3]. *Mercurius Politicus* (8-15 Aug. 1650), p.172. E. 609 [13]. L. Curelly, '"The French, those Monkies of Mankind": the Fronde as seen by the newsbook *Mercurius Politicus*', *XVII-XVIII: Revue de la Société d'études anglo-américaines des XVII*[e] *et SVIII*[e] *siècles*, 69 (2012), pp.29-50. L. Curelly and N. Smith, Introduction, to L. Curelly and N. Smith (eds.), *Radical Voices, Radical Ways* (Manchester, MUP, 2016), p.22. I am grateful to Ariel Hessayon for this reference.

Thus Sexby came to be out of a profession in the early 1650s.

The English Republic was looking for allies and certainly had no qualms about promoting internal problems for the French monarchy, which refused to recognise it. The Council of State, specifically its secret committee dealing with French affairs, sent a delegation to France. Marten had been receiving news about events in France since 1650 at least, and Cromwell and Marten were members of the committee. They alighted on Sexby as the leader of a group of envoys that included Sexby's servant Samuel Dyer, Thomas Arundell, John Tubbing, and quite possibly Leveller Richard Overton. Marten was no doubt ideologically sympathetic to Sexby, Cromwell may have chosen Sexby from a mixture of feelings of old comradeship and desire to have such a critical and independent spirit engaged in useful work beyond England's shores. And so it was that Sexby set sail from England headed for Bordeaux in the summer of 1651 instructed to 'to give an account of the state of the country and affections of the people'. Supplied with a grant of £1,000 a year for his delegation, it would be a month short of two years before he returned. Every two weeks, a letter reporting his activities was sent back to Thomas Scot, chief intelligencer of the Council of State. He also sent letters of intelligence to Henry Marten, suggesting in one that they write in invisible ink in the lines between the visible text of their correspondence.[6]

---

[6] *CSPD: Interregnum, 1654*, pp.139-94. C. H. Firth, 'Thomas Scot's Account of his Actions as Intelligencer during the Commonwealth', *English Historical Review*, Vol. XII, Issue XLV (Jan. 1897), pp.119-120. P. A. Knachbel, *England and the Fronde, The Impact of the English Civil War and Revolution in France* (New York, Cornell University Press, 1967), p.161. HMC, 'The manuscripts of Capt. F.C. Loder-Symonds', in *The Manuscripts of Rye and Hereford Corporations, etc. Thirteenth Report, Appendix: Part IV* (London, 1892), pp.378-404. *State Papers of John Thurloe, Vol. 6, January 1657- March 1658* (London, 1742), pp.823-36. The suggestion that Overton was part of the delegation is made in J. Holstun, *Ehud's Dagger: Class Struggle in the English Revolution* (London, Verso Books, 2000), pp.310-11. Holston relies on Marmaduke Langdale's letter of 20 September 1655, part of exchanges about continental Royalist intrigues with the Levellers. What the letter asserts beyond question is that Overton

Among the *Ormee*, Sexby found himself in congenial company. In September 1652, using the pseudonym Stephen Edwards, Sexby wrote to Marten, whom he addressed as 'truth's solicitor' and 'liberty's champion', imploring him to not to reinforce the errors of the English Republic by failing to support the Ormee:

> 'Tis to be lamented his many prizes have been put in your hands, [and] what hath not been weakly managed hath been covetously monopolized: now you have another ball thrown to you ... [T]he people's score is the best and safest interest to come in upon and this when you are fit to hear shall be spoken loud enough - 'Oh England come and help your laws shall be ours.'

---

and Sexby (going by the alias Mr. Brooke) were closely in touch in this period, that Overton was 'imployed by Cromwell amongest the Hugonetts in France', and that Overton had 'brought a paper under thowsand of there handes to Cromwell to invite him to sende some forces into France to joine with them to assert there privileges.' These forces are very likely to have been the ones discussed in respect of English military assistance to the Bordeaux republic. Although this correspondence dates from after the events in Bordeaux, it seems likely they refer to them. In December 1653, Overton was paid £20 for his services by spymaster John Thurloe, which may well have been for the mission described in the Langdale letter. In summary, Holston is justified in concluding that Overton may have been directly one of Sexby's delegation or, at the very least, at work on the same project and in touch with Sexby. Overton's participation would also be an important factor explaining the Bordeaux republicans' adoption of *The Agreement of the People*. See, G. F. Warner, *The Nicholas Papers* (London, Camden Society, 1897), pp.43-5, 50-5. 'Richard Overton', *ODNB*. We owe the suggestion that Cromwell was minded to remove Sexby because of Sexby's critical views of the new regime to Ludlow. But Ludlow seems to muddle the timeline of Sexby's departure in 1651 for France and his specific support for Ludlow's own criticisms of the regime in the petitions and the 'Momento' in 1654. Nevertheless, it is possible that Sexby's critical views were apparent earlier and that these played a part in Cromwell's support for his engagement overseas. E. Ludlow, *The Memoirs of Edmund Ludlow*, Vol. I, pp. 406-15.

In May 1653, Sexby wrote to his masters in England urging support for the *Ormee*, telling them: 'Tis pity to lose so glorious an opportunity to serve the church of God, and free millions from slavery.' Sexby oversaw the translation and publication of the Levellers' last 1649 *Agreement of the People* in French. It was a free rendering of that document, not fully adapted to its new setting, but it was accompanied by an equally radical *Manifeste*. This latter document contained the sentiment that, 'The peasant is as free as the prince, for he comes into the world with neither sabots on his feet nor a saddle on his back - no more than the child of a king is born with a golden crown on his head.' This was a French version of a sentiment first expressed in John Harris' *Mercurius Militaris*, the short-lived Leveller paper aimed at the New Model Army rank and file, and spoken again by Leveller Richard Rumbold on his scaffold in the 1660s: 'none comes into the world with a saddle upon his back, neither any booted and spurred to ride him'. From there made it on to pages written by Thomas Jefferson and Daniel Defoe. But in Bordeaux itself the cause was lost, leaving *Mercurius Politicus* to mourn the sight of the red flags removed from the church spires and the green ribbons removed from the arms of the rebels to be replaced with the white flags of surrender: 'the chiefe Townsmen threw down the red clothes, or colours of the Elmers from the Steples, and to signifie the intentions of this Assembly, they took away the green ribands, and took white, and placed also the white clothes or colours upon the Steeples….'[7]

Edward Sexby's mission to Bordeaux, though fascinating, is a

---

[7] S. A. Westrich, *The Ormee of Bordeaux, A Revolution during the Fronde* (Baltimore, John Hopkins University Press, 1972), p.22. *State Papers of John Thurloe, Volume 1, 1638-1653*, pp.237-50. E. Vernon and P. Baker, 'Appendix I, *Les principes, fondement et gouverement d'une republique:* The French *Agreement of the People*', in E. Vernon and P. Baker, *The Agreements of the People, The Levellers, and the Constitutional Crisis of the English Revolution* (London, Palgrave Macmillan, 2012), pp.262-6. J. Holstun, *Ehud's dagger*, pp.310-11. J. Rees, *The Leveller Revolution* (London, Verso, 2016), p.258. *Mercurius Politicus* (21-28 July 1653), p.2604. E. 708 [2].

mere incident in the long arc of the English Revolution. But it is an incident that begs much larger questions. As historian Carlo Ginzburg has recently observed, 'In history as in cinema, every close-up implies an off-screen scene':

> 'Working on a case in an analytical way is close to this. But, of course, you also have to take into account the off-screen, otherwise the close-up would not make sense. This implies that in any close-up the global perspective is implicit. Every singular case assumes the possibility of a generalisation, and there is a back and forth between the one and the other.[8]

This is very true of Sexby's experience with the *Ormee*. One very large question that emerges from this smaller story is why the English were able to make a successful revolution where the French failed. And that question becomes even larger when both the English revolution and the revolt of *Ormee* are seen in the context of other revolts in Europe that exploded in the 1640s: the Reapers' War in Catalonia in 1640-41, the Naples rebellion of 1647, the revolt in Sicily the same year. Taken together, one historian observes 'the middle of the seventeenth century saw revolutions more widespread than at any other time except in 1848'.[9]

---

[8] C. Ginzburg, 'In history as in cinema, every close-up implies an off-screen scene', Verso blog, available at https://tinyurl.com/2axxrerc

[9] H. G. Koenigsberger, 'The Revolt of Palermo in 1647', *The Cambridge Historical Journal*, Vol.8, No.3 (1946), p.130. A point repeated by G. Parker and L. M. Smith in the introduction to G. Parker and L. M. Smith (eds.), *The General Crisis of the Seventeenth Century* (London, Routledge, Kegan, Paul, 1978), p.20: '1848 resembled 1648 in so many ways'. I do not intend to revisit the debate about the general crisis of the seventeenth century here, although I make use of some of the insights of those historians who contributed to that long and ongoing discussion. My focus is more narrowly on those revolts which have the closest parallel with events in England and to operate in a more restricted frame of determination. Part of the problem with the general-crisis debate is that some of the discussion takes place at such a level of generality that it fails to explain specifically the course of events, or at least not without

II

The revolts in Catalonia, Naples, and Palermo were all linked to the crisis of the Spanish monarchy at the close of the Thirty Years War. All three territories were ruled by Spain and in all these territories an increase in taxes to pay for Madrid's military exploits in Europe were the trigger for popular resistance. In Catalonia long-term regional scepticism about attempts to integrate the region into a more centralised Spanish monarchy were hugely exacerbated by conflicts over the billeting of troops on the local population. Felipe IV ascended to the throne in 1621, four years before Charles I was crowned in England. He appointed his favourite, Count-Duke Gaspar de Guzmán Olivares, as effective first minister, just as Charles anointed the Duke of Buckingham. In 1626, Olivares introduced the *Union de armas*, the Union of Arms, an empire-wide attempt to raise an army for European wars. Olivares knew the scheme was a dangerous gamble. He wrote, 'to my mind this will lose everything irremediably or save the ship. Here go religion, king, kingdom, nation, everything…'. Catalonia was to pay for 16,000 conscripts. Felipe made an insultingly brief visit to the Catalonian *Corts*, the first he had called in 27 years, but failed to get their agreement to the levy. A second *Corts* convened by Olivares in 1632 also ended in stalemate. Olivares proceeded without agreement. In 1635, France declared war on Spain and Olivares took advantage of the opportunity this provided to occupy Catalonia and impose the Union of Arms. As Sir Arthur Hopton, English resident in Madrid, friend of Olivares, and uncle to Ralph Hopton, the Royalist general of the English Civil War, wrote, 'the people of Cataluna begin to suspect that under colour of service against the French, these forces are to be employed to reduce them to reason.' Some 40,000 soldiers that Spain sent to confront the French at the border were billeted on the Catalans. There was widespread resistance to the inevitable depredations of the troops and the

---

further mediation. The origins of the debate lie in articles printed in *Past & Present*, first collected in T. H. Aston (ed.), *Crisis in Europe 1560-1660* (London, RKP, 1965). For a more recent restatement see, G. Parker, 'Crisis and Catastrophe: The Global Crisis of the Seventeenth Century Reconsidered', *The American Historical Review*, pp.1053-79.

reports read exactly like the accounts of riots and disturbances over billeting experienced by Charles I and the Duke of Buckingham in the late 1620s.[10]

The situation was already at boiling point when the French successfully took Salces in northern Catalonia in 1639. It was retaken in January 1640, but the Catalans saw this as their, costly, victory not that of Olivares' troops. The revolt against billeting grew. By May, some towns were refusing to allow troops to enter, leaving them to fend for themselves beyond the walls. Then a householder in the town of Santa Coloma de Farners drew his pistol and shot dead the arrogant, drunken officer responsible for billeting. On 14 May, the military burnt the town down. This, in turn, sparked province-wide riots. On 22 May, a crowd of some 200 swept into Barcelona to free Francesca Tamarit, a hero of the battle of Salces and a prominent critic of army abuses in Catalonia. They called out 'Long live the King!' and 'Down with bad government!', headed to the prison and pulled down its gates. The revolt was now widespread with protestors arriving at town gates admitted by sympathisers within the walls. This was followed by the sacking of the homes of the rich. 'The rebellion', writes J. H. Elliott, 'swept to and fro across north Catalonia, unresisted, irresistible'.[11]

The rebellion became a full-blown insurrection on 7 June 1640, Corpus Christi Day. This was the traditional start of the harvest and there were some hundreds of reapers on Barcelona's Ramblas waiting to be hired. Each carried their sickle. One of their number was injured in an incident with soldiers. It was enough to ignite widespread rioting. The reapers were joined by the city poor and they sacked the houses of the wealthy, heaping the luxurious contents on to bonfires in the streets, and crying out 'Long Live our Land!' and

[10] J. H. Elliott, *The Revolt of the Catalans, A Study in the Decline of Spain 1598-1640* (Cambridge, CUP, 1963), pp.283, 310, and ch.XV. J. H. Elliott, 'Revolts in the Spanish Monarchy' in R. Forster and J. P. Greene, *Preconditions of Revolution in Early Modern Europe* (Baltimore, John Hopkins Press, 1970), ch.3. M. Eaude, *A People's History of Catalonia* (London, Pluto, 2022), pp.53-6. P. Anderson, *Lineages of the Absolutist State* (London, Verso, 1974), pp.79-82.

[11] J. H. Elliott, *The Revolt of the Catalans*, pp.419-20, 428-33, 448-9.

'Death to the Traitors!'. Members of the city council, the *Generalitat*, tried to calm the crowd. The tension was too much for one councillor who collapsed under the strain. The rumour spread that soldiers were responsible. The crowd headed to the shipbuilding area where the King's viceroy, the Count of Santa Coloma, was hoping to be rescued by ship. As he and his remaining escort fled along the beach, they were bombarded by stones and musket fire and hacked down by the sickles of the reapers pursuing them. Santa Coloma died from a dagger thrust into his stomach by one of the reapers. This was the signal for widespread attacks on judges, royal officials, and the wealthy, not just in Barcelona, but throughout Catalonia. In England, one report told of 'a notable mutiny in Catalonia' in which 'the people have killed divers of the King's soldiers there garrisoned, and the Viceroy himself is shot with a pistol.' Another recorded that 'in Catalonia 6,000 Spanish soldiers were cut to pieces whom the Spaniards had sent to quarter there; but ... they [the Catalans] allege they were compelled to fall upon them for their own security, which the King of Spain will not put up with, knowing the Catalonians bear a most inveterate hatred to the Castilians.'[12]

The King was certainly stunned by the death of Santa Coloma. He wrote that it was 'the like of which has never been seen in any province or kingdom of the world.' Olivares rent his clothes when he heard the news. His policies as well as his garments were in tatters. He was reading reports from his own allies which stressed, 'The peasants are so roused that as long as billeting continues they will not hesitate to face any danger to save themselves from the injuries, insults, sacrilege and devastation of their homes by the soldiers.' Olivares was too weak, and the insurrection at that moment too powerful, for immediate repression. Many around the King, nevertheless, advocated it. But Olivares played for time. In England there were those that wished Charles I would adopt the same policy with the Scots: 'the King of Spain offers his rebels of Catalonia to sign a

---

[12] Eaude, *A People's History of Catalonia*, pp.55-6. Sir George Radcliff to Edward Lord Conway, and Edmund Rossingham to Edward Viscount Conway in CSPD: Charles I, 1640, (London, 1880), pp.258-91, 434-74.

blank and let them write what conditions they would have; we wish the Scots out again and in their own territory on those terms rather than to hazard our lives and fortunes where nothing is to be got but wounds and death, all which we must expose now to drive these rebels out again.'

By August, the *Generalitat* convened a new, expanded assembly in which artisans and merchants had much greater sway. It broke decisively with the Spanish King and took control of the royal arsenal. The Catalans concluded a treaty with the French, an arrangement encouraged by the Catalan rich as a bulwark against popular radicalism. But there was also a well-founded fear in all classes that the Spanish crown would seek retribution as soon as practicable. But the cost of the French alliance was that the new Republic was short lived. French help meant the recognition of Louis XIII as Count of Barcelona. In late October, Olivares sent an army of 24,000 into the south of Catalonia. Tortosa and Tarragona collapsed and swore their loyalty to the Crown. That mattered little; reprisals were widespread and brutal. The Royalist army cut a bloody swathe through Catalonia as it headed north to Barcelona. They were checked at the battle of Montjuic on 26 January by a force of Catalan volunteers and French troops. The Spanish defeat helped end Olivares' career, but the French troops came to stay and were soon as unpopular as the Spanish troops had been. French generals took over the lands deserted by Spanish landowners now sheltering in Madrid. By 1652, revolts against the French were favouring Felipe IV. Eventually, in the 1659 Treaty of the Pyrenees, Spain and Catalonia lost land to France and what remained of Catalonia was back under the Spanish Crown.[13]

In Naples, the third largest city in Europe at the time, the aristocrats attempted to impose a new tax on fruit in order to finance the exactions of the Spanish monarchy. A young fisherman, Tommaso

---

[13] J. H. Elliott, *The Revolt of the Catalans*, pp.435, 452. Edmund Rossingham to Edward Viscount Conway in *CSPD*: Charles I, 1640-1 (London, 1882) pp.88-127. Eaude, *A People's History of Catalonia*, pp.57-9. P. Anderson, *Lineages of the Absolutist State*, pp.80-1. R. B. Merriman, *Six Contemporaneous Revolutions*, pp.1-11.

Aneillo d'Amalfi, known as Masaniello, led the protests which began in July 1647 with a riot at the city gates between fruit sellers and customs officers. The crowd then drove the Spanish viceroy, the Duke of Arcos, from his home. The rioters armed themselves by ransacking armouries and threw open the prisons. Masaniello demanded parity between the people and the nobility. This phase of the rebellion succeeded when the viceroy pardoned the rebels, allowed some citizens to bear arms, and removed the harshest taxes. Masaniello himself was assassinated just ten days into the revolt. After Spanish ships bombarded the city, a second wave of revolt in August aimed at Spain as well as the local nobility was led by local gunsmith Gennaro Annese. The Spanish viceroy's army was expelled and a Republic declared in October 1647. The rebels offered to make Henry, Duke of Guise, constitutional monarch in order to secure French support. In emulation of the ancient Roman republic, the rebels adopted a coat of arms adorned with both Guise's heraldic devices and the legend SPQN, standing for The Senate and People of Naples, although the alternate description of *Reale Repubblica*, the Royal Republic, caught the contradictory reality more fully. The Duke of Guise made his aims painfully clear in his later memoirs: 'My intention has always been to re-establish order and to subject them [the people of Naples] once more to authority of the nobility'. The alliance with the Duke immediately embroiled the new Republic in warfare between French and Spanish forces. By the summer of the following year, 1648, the Spanish eventually triumphed and Gennaro Annese was beheaded in the Piazza del Mercato where the revolt began.[14]

The Naples rebellion did not have the direct involvement of English parliamentarians in the way that Sexby and Overton were engaged in events in Bordeaux. But English radicals certainly did follow events in Naples with interest and drew appropriate lessons. The writer and publisher John Dillingham, a close associate of Oliver Cromwell, kept readers of his *The Moderate Intelligencer* well

---

[14] R. Villari, *The Revolt of Naples* (Oxford, Polity, 1993) p.135. D. Boerio, 'The "Trouble in Naples" in the Political Information Arena of the English Revolution', in J. Raymond and N. Moxham, *News Networks in Early Modern Europe* (Leiden, Brill, 2016), p.779.

informed about the Neapolitan rebellion week by week as events unfolded. In the nineteen weeks from December 1647 to May 1648, news of the revolt in Naples occupied on average four pages of *The Moderate Intelligencer*, almost a third of its content. Dillingham parted company with his printer Robert White in mid-1648, and White went on to print the Leveller paper *The Moderate*. Reports continued in Dillingham's next issue. In its first issue, *The Moderate* also took up the story of the repression of the rebellion, reporting on the 220 Citizens who had been jailed and on the beheading of Gennaro Annese. At the height of revolutionary agitation in November 1647 in London, 150 weavers meeting at the Mouth Inn, a frequent haunt of Levellers, considered if they should follow the example of Naples where the speaker believed, 'The same Business we are upon is perfected in Naples; for if any Person stand up for Monarchie there, he is immediately hanged at the Doore'. By May 1648 there was a loyalist account in print of what, in an unusual modern usage, it described as a 'revolution'. The following year there was 77-page pamphlet, *The Rebellion of Naples or the Tragedy of Massenello*, presented as a playscript.[15]

In January 1648, the Commons printed a *Declaration* justifying breaking off negotiations with the King, the Vote of No Addresses. The example of 'the late bloody violation of the Peace betwixt the Crown of Spain, and those of Naples', MPs wrote, 'is so fresh in our memories' as an example that no 'Prince once ingaged in a War with his Subjects … ever kept to any Agreement he made with them' that they could not 'expect that any Propositions agreed upon at the Isle of Wight, should binde the King more'. *The Royal Project*, the work

---

[15] D. Boerio, 'The "Trouble in Naples" in the Political Information Arena of the English Revolution', pp.779-804. R. Villari, *The Revolt of Naples*; Villari records that the revolution in Naples 'had an immense resonance throughout Europe', p.181. J. Rees, *The Leveller Revolution*, p.56. *The Moderate*, No.1 (10-17 June 1648) pp.4-5. E. 454 [2]. *The Moderate*, No.2 (17-24 June 1648) p.13. E. 453 [8]. *A True Relation of the reducing of the The City of Naples To the Obedience of the King of Spaine* (London, 1648) p.1. E. 438 [18]. *The Rebellion of Naples or the Tragedy of Massenello* (London, 1649), B199 (Wing).

of the pseudonymous Verity Victor, used Leveller-inflected language to denounce the 'perfidious King of Spain' who 'had granted whatsoever' 'the people of Naples' demanded. But once he 'regained his power' he 'put multitudes of the principal men of Naples, that had been most active and zealous for the people, and publike liberties, to death.' In *The Tenure of Kings and Magistrates*, John Milton cited the rebellion 'this very year in Naples' as an example of the disasters that would befall any people that did not recognise 'the perfidious cruelty' that has been used 'as a constant maxim of state' by the Spanish kings 'on their subjects that have taken arms, and after trusted them'. John Cook, prosecutor in the King's trial, cited the execution of corn speculators in the Naples rebellion as an example of the application of the Law of Nature and Reason even 'when our Law Books are silent'. In 1649, John Goodwin quoted the Commons *Declaration* of 1648 to justify the execution of the King.[16]

The revolt in Palermo happened in exactly the same timeframe as the Neapolitan rebellion and for broadly similar reasons, though its impact on English politics was far more restricted. Like Naples, Sicily was a possession of the Spanish crown, ruled by a Spanish viceroy answerable to Madrid. The costs of war had, as in Naples, led Madrid was putting 'unbearable financial burdens on the lower classes or infringing the political privileges of aristocracies and commercial middle classes in traditionally autonomous States, in its efforts to create a centralized Spanish State'. The subsistence farming of the peasantry was hit by a poor harvest in the autumn of 1646 and by torrential rains in the spring of 1647. The authorities tried to ameliorate the effects of this by subsidising the cost of bread, but on 8 May 1647 they reduced the size of loaves. Crowds, many of them women, held up the miserable portions of bread, crying in the street.

---

[16] *Declaration of the Commons of England* (London, 1648), p.13. E. 528 [23]. V. Verity, *The Royal Project* (London, 1648), p.13. E. 468 [22]. J. Milton, *The Tenure of Kings and Magistrates* in S. Orgel and J. Goldberg (eds.), *John Milton* (Oxford, OUP, 1991), p.298. J. Cook, *King Charls his Case* (London, 1649), pp.27-8, C6025 (Wing). J. Goodwin, *Hybristodkai, The Obstuctours of Justice* (London, 1649), p.124, E. 572 [2]. A royalist pamphlet justified Kingly duplicity toward rebels in order to regain power, see *A Letter Sent form Newport* (1648), p.3. E 464 [29].

Then sorrow turned to anger. Riots took place at the palace gates, which were then burned down. Monks had to protect the houses of the most unpopular Senators. Prisoners were freed from jail. The crowds chanted, as they had done in Catalonia and Naples, 'Long live the King and down with taxes and bad government'.[17]

The crowds were largely lower class and found their first leader in the huge miller, Antonino La Pilosa. By 20 May, they had turned their anger on tax offices and the treasury. The Viceroy gave ground. Loaves were restored to their previous size and the hated 'five gabelles' (taxes on grain, wine, oil, meat, and cheese) were abolished. Moreover, escaped prisoners were granted amnesty and the people were given the right to elect two so-called Popular Senators. This last concession was probably aimed at the artisan guilds who now took over control of Palermo's fortifications. The elected senators, Francesco Salerno and Simone Sabatini, were both rich merchants more sympathetic to the aristocracy than the people and open to compromise with the Viceroy. This, however, did not yet prevent the spread of the revolution through Sicily during June and July. Only Messina seemed untouched by the revolt. In July, news of events in Naples made Masaniello's name as famous in Palermo as it was in his native city. A more substantial link between the two rebellions was the return from Naples of former prisoner and gold-beater Giuseppe d'Alesi. He headed for the densely packed Tanner's district of Palermo where the tunnels that led from house to house made the area an ideal centre of revolutionary organisation. Here d'Alesi and his fellows planned the overthrow of the Viceroy, his ministers, and the nobility.[18]

Rumours that the Viceroy had taken the Popular Senators captive were enough to spark a new wave of protest. On 15 August, riots once again swept towards the palace, the crowd only turned aside by the Spanish guard. Undeterred, d'Alesi, dressed in white armour and on horseback, led the crowd in storming the Senate armouries and the custom houses. The Viceroy fled to a ship in the harbour, the nobles to their country estates. But the revolution had no executive capacity

---

[17] H. G. Koenigsberger, 'The Revolt of Palermo in 1647', *The Cambridge Historical Journal*, Vol.8, No.3 (1946), pp.130-3.
[18] ibid. pp.133-6.

and it was negotiation with the Viceroy that resulted in the granting of 49 laws, or *Capitoli*, which included tax reductions for the poor and amnesties for the rioters, reform of government to allow greater guild participation, and legal reform which appeased the lawyers and intellectuals that had attached themselves to the movement. But the agreement also re-confirmed the Viceroy's position and this concession fatally undermined d'Alesi's authority with the masses.

The day after the Viceroy signed the *Capitoli*, 22 August, d'Alesi's house in the Tanner's quarter was stormed by two columns of counterrevolutionaries, one organised by the nobles and the other by the fishermens' guild. They brutally murdered d'Alesi, his brother, and a dozen of his compatriots. But the Viceroy overplayed his hand by attempting to arrest the popular consuls. The cry went up 'Serra, Serra - To the Barricades', and rumours spread that d'Alesi was once again astride his horse in white armour. The Viceroy retreated, the consuls were released and the *Capitoli* reconfirmed. However, this was the rebellion's last hurrah. Unable to generate a stable Sicily-wide governmental structure and with its best-known leader dead, the authorities clawed back their power. By mid-September, the always weak support of the guilds had turned into a petition to the Viceroy to repeal the *Capitoli* 'as being originated by the rebel Alesi and without public usefulness'.[19]

III

So what can we say about the differences between the successful English revolution and the defeated European rebellions in Catalonia, Bordeaux, Naples and Palermo? In Catalonia, there are a number of distinct features to the revolution. In the first place, although the revolt was often driven by the anger and actions of the poorest, it was not this section of society that determined what the outcomes would be; in this sense they were much more like peasant revolts than the actions of the London crowd which drove forward the English Revolution in its crucial stages. Indeed, the revolt spread from the countryside to Barcelona which was relatively quiescent

---

[19] ibid. pp.136-40.

in the early stages of the rebellion. One reason for this is that the urban middling sort and merchants were overridingly concerned with issues of Catalonian independence. 'For the Catalan commercial classes', writes J. H. Elliott, 'no particular advantage was to be gained from breaking free from the Monarchy; it was enough to keep Castile at arm's length.' When the popular rising had driven out Spanish troops and tax collectors, its wrath began to turn on the oligarchs and the rich who had replaced them. The threat of Spanish reconquest produced fear among Catalans, but it also provided the more conservative commercial classes and the oligarchs with the best possible reason for the French alliance and the re-establishment of a monarchical regime.[20]

In Bordeaux, the red flag was a portent of things to come, but it was not yet an icon with real historical force behind it. In England, Charles' attempt to reconstruct the state on absolutist lines ran into very substantial social forces unwilling to countenance that project. In France, the Fronde was less a single revolution than it was a series of rebellions, a rebellion of aristocrats, of the *Parlement*, of the bourgeoisie, and of the peasants and the poor. 'Each with grievances of their own', writes Merriman, 'they could not – perhaps one may safely say they would not – effectively combine against the Crown.' Moreover, Bordeaux was not France and the *Ormee* were not the whole of the Fronde. The gentry in France were not rulers of their counties, nor were they so involved in agricultural markets or related economically and socially to urban merchants. The *Parlement* in Paris was a gathering of lawyers at court, not a gentry-dominated legislative assembly. French society and the French aristocracy were more feudal, less hollowed out by the growth of markets, than their English counterparts. No Reformation had destroyed the Catholic church and so the corrosive presence of Puritanism was limited to minorities, it was not a national religion internalising debate about the direction of church and state. Some elements of the Fronde echoed civil-war England, but perhaps as much the civil war of Yorkists versus Lancastrians as that of Parliamentarians versus Royalists. Only in Bordeaux was the rebellion able to shake itself free of a leadership dominated by internecine

---

[20] J. H. Elliott, 'Revolts in the Spanish Monarchy', p.120.

aristocratic struggles. But even here, at least in *Mercurius Politicus*' view, it was internal division and the influence of Presbyterian-like moderates which were part of the cause of defeat: 'the Parliament of Bordeaux hath found out the old knack of England, and intended to play over our game for King and Parliament, reserving a little cranie still in the Conscience, for that fawning cur, which some call Loyalty though it be but contented Slavery.' The petite Fronde, or the Fronde of the Princes, was threatened by the large Fronde '"emerging from the common people, or at least from the very small bourgeoise, although it also had members in the highest ranks" and counting in its fold, the "most violent" members'.[21]

Some modern accounts agree: the parliamentary and noble leadership of the Fronde 'took great care not to commit themselves, or to be committed to social revolution.' Republicans in France, unlike their English counterparts, did not succeed in binding together a political bloc of lower gentry and middling sort that could ultimately take state power. They were divided, isolated, and defeated in Bordeaux, their popular leaders escaped death in English exile, though one was racked and broken under the elms. The French monarchy continued developing on absolutist lines, simultaneously encouraged by its victory and still fearful of revolt from below. It would not be until 1789 that the French were successfully to challenge their ruling monarchy and aristocracy. And when they did, Sexby's prose, the incendiary pamphlet justifying tyrannicide, *Killing Noe Murder*, appeared again in French translation.[22]

---

[21] R. B. Merriman, *Six Contemporaneous Revolutions*, p.50. *Mercurius Politicus* (18-25 July 1650), p.105, E. 608 [11]. L. Curelly, quoting from correspondence of 1652, in '"Do look on the other side of the water": Cromwell's foreign policy towards France', para. 3, e-Rea [Online], 11.2 | 2014, posted online on July 15, 2014, consulted on April 22, 2024. URL: http://journals.openedition.org/erea/3751; M. Fulbrook, 'The English Revolution and the Revisionist Revolt', *Social History*, Vol. 7, No. 3 (Oct. 1982) pp. 254-5.

[22] A. Lloyd Moote, 'The Preconditions of Revolution' in G. Parker and L. M. Smith, *The General Crisis of the Seventeenth Century*, p.140. L. Curelly and N. Smith, Introduction, to L. Curelly and N. Smith (eds.), *Radical Voices, Radical Ways*, p.23.

In Naples and Palermo, the most advanced notion of a political settlement was the idea of a mixed monarchy. In other words, the Italian radicals arrived at the end of the revolution where the English parliamentarians were at the opening of the Long Parliament. There were no significant numbers of fiery spirited republicans or Levellers who emerged during the course of the events in Naples or Palermo. This was partly a product of the social context. 'The interests of the merchant bourgeoisie in the towns, which was more Catalan and Genoese than Sicilian, approximated those of the nobility to whose ranks they were always hoping to be raised.' The guilds were still mired in their feudal formation, the national state could not be conquered and used as an engine of revolution. Of the Palermo rebellion, H. G. Koenigsberger notes,

> The most immediate reason for the failure of the revolution was the impossibility of establishing a revolutionary constitution with the co-operation of people and nobles in the Government. Yet for a complete overthrow of the social order the revolutionary forces were not strong enough. The Sicilian revolutionaries had almost none of the advantages of the contemporary English Parliamentarians. They did not represent a rising class of prosperous country gentlemen and capitalist merchants; they had no leaders of the calibre of Pym and Cromwell, educated men, schooled by long experience of political life and not handicapped by social inferiority. They lacked the great moral strength which the English Puritans drew from their religious beliefs – in harmony with their political aspirations. Though no less religious, the Sicilians found that their religion became the strongest weapon in the hands of the established order. The Sicilian revolution was never backed by a consistent political philosophy.[23]

Italian Marxist Rosario Villari makes some similar points in his pathbreaking study of the Naples revolt. He notes that in Naples, as well as in Catalonia and Palermo, 'one of the immediate causes

---

[23] H. G. Koenigsberger, 'The Revolt of Palermo in 1647', *The Cambridge Historical Journal*, Vol.8, No.3 (1946), pp.130-1, 144.

of the irremediable internal division was the fact that the increasing tax burden was accompanied by the concession of increasingly wide "liberty" to the aristocracy.' This ensured that 'there was not even a temporary convergence of political and social forces' like that which occurred in the opening phases of the English Revolution. Such differences as there were between Spain and the aristocracy were marginal and 'solidarity between the monarchy and the baronage remained firm throughout the history of the viceroyalty and was permanently sealed when the revolution of 1647 made apparent the political direction in which the kingdom was actually headed.' In England, the rupture within the aristocracy opened a space in which more radical projects grew. In the later phases of the English case the 'the greater importance of the religious factor in England was responsible for the flowering of radical and extremist tendencies in the movement.' But radicalism took hold in England when a divided landowning class was weakened, but in Naples the alliance with the Duke of Guise and the nobles' loyalty to Spain provided much less propitious circumstances.[24]

The purpose of this chapter has not been to provide a rounded account of the European revolutions of the mid-seventeenth century. It has merely been to draw attention to their existence and to suggest that this fact inevitably poses questions of causality both in each specific case and in comparison with the English Revolution. 'France had its Frondes, which were important social movements; Catalan, Neapolitan and Portuguese revolutions marked the crisis of the Spanish Empire in the 1640s', wrote Eric Hobsbawm, but beyond the Dutch and the English 'with their new, and experimental bourgeois regimes most of Europe found an efficient and stable form of government in absolutism on the French model.' This, in short, is the Edward Sexby question: why did these revolutions occur and what accounts for their successes and failures? The only further observation here is that it is implausible to suggest that we can answer this question without looking at the long-term development of economic forces, class formations, and state structure which are a part of them. These clearly separated English from French, Ital-

[24] R. Villari, *The Revolt of Naples*, pp.125-6, 174.

ian or Catalan experiences. It was because the class forces to which they were attached and the economic circumstances of those classes were very different that similar republican ideas had very different levels of development and political consequences on either side of the English Channel. In this context, Hobsbawm makes a vital, and entirely orthodox Marxist, point:

> 'It is sometimes assumed that the development of a 'capitalist class' and of the elements of the capitalist mode of production within feudal society automatically produce these conditions. In the long run, taking the widest view over the centuries from 1000 to 1800 this is no doubt so. In the shorter run it is not. Unless certain conditions are present – it is by no means yet clear what they are – the scope of capitalist expansion will be limited by the prevalence of the feudal structure....'[25]

This indeterminacy reinforces rather than undermines the importance of politics to the historical outcomes. English socio-economic and state development presented English revolutionaries with possibilities not open to those on the continent. But that does not mean that the possibilities were necessarily going to be realised. Opportunities opened up by socio-economic developments could have been lost in the political register. Similarly, even where socio-economic possibilities were more restricted, a range of political alternatives were still open. Olivares' gamble aimed at constructing a unified Spanish absolutism was not necessarily doomed to failure. Political choices by Spanish monarchists and Catalan, Neapolitan, and Sicilian revolutionaries ensured that outcome. In other work, particularly *The Leveller Revolution* and *The Fiery Spirits*, I have concentrated on the political forces that shaped the English Revolution. In these essays I look at the class formations in England in the mid-seventeenth century and how they were expressed in a variety of, often clashing, political projects.

---

[25] E. Hobsbawm, 'The General Crisis of the European Economy in the 17th Century', *Past & Present*, No.5, (May 1954), pp.37-40.

Chapter 2

Politics and class in the English Revolution

The relationship between politics, the broader class profile of society, and the socio-economic structure of mid-seventeenth-century England is highly contentious. Class is automatically assumed by some to lead to a reductionist or teleological analysis. The long shadow of the revisionist attempt to extirpate Marxism from the study of the English Revolution made sensible discussion of this issue almost impossible for some decades. But now some useful ground has been cleared in this respect by John Morrill's recent re-examination of what is living and what is dead in the revisionist canon. We can largely leave the past of revisionism behind here for there is enough work to do going forward in, one hopes, a Walwynian spirit of reasoned discussion.

Perhaps the most important point that emerges from Morrill's account of what he calls the 'revisionist moment' is that, in the end, a reconsideration of the longer and deeper causes of the English Revolution became necessary once more. Morrill records that by the 1990s both he and Conrad Russell 'had come round to the view that there was an efficient cause of the civil wars of the 1640s, the religious policy of Charles I and the response it evoked: radical religion.' And, up to a point, we can all say amen to that. But only up to a point, because, and this is a contention of revisionism that it shares with Marxism, if politics has 'its own structures and patterns that were irreducible to other things', then one of the other things that it is not reducible to is religion. Economic reductionism is not the only kind of reductionism. Better, surely, to frame class structure and religion, and their relation, as contextually indispensable for understanding political conflicts without making politics reducible to either. This model, long known as a mediated totality in the Marxist tradition, provides exactly what Morrill rightly seems intent on preserving: a non-determinist account of politics. He aims at an account which combines 'how the past has shaped the present with attempts to enter into the material and, more particularly, the mental worlds of the past, to see how men and women made sense of the world they lived in.' This would be account in which 'people make choices and articulate those choices in specific personal and group circumstances.'[1]

This formulation of Morrill's has a welcome and familiar ring to those who have read Marx. It rather sounds as if Morrill is directly addressing a point made by Mary Fulbrook in an early response to revisionism:

> Revisionists have so far failed to come to terms in any explicit and satisfactory way with the truth of Marx's dictum that 'Men make their own history, but they do not make it as the please; they do not make it under circumstances chosen by themselves, but under circumstances directly encountered, give and transmitted from the past.' Attempting to avoid both the Scylla of teleological determinism and the Charybdis of anachronistic revolutionary free-will, the revisionists run the risk of shipwreck in a sea of confusion and largely negative assertions.

Indeed, the whole point of Marx's 'men make history, but not

---

[1] J. Morrill, 'Revisionism's Wounded Legacies', *Huntington Library Quarterly*, Vol.78, No.4 (Winter 2015), pp.577-94, specifically pp.588, 592-3. K. Marx, 'Theses on Feuerbach' in *Early Writings* (London, Penguin, 1974), pp.421-4. Of course, there is a journalistic and academic industry devoted to proving that Marxism is determinism, but it should at least be acknowledged that the main line of descent in Western Marxism from Marx and Engels through Luxemburg, Lukács, and Gramsci (who, pace Morrill, p.584, was a Marxist) is radically anti-determinist in its philosophical stance. There have been Marxists who are determinists, Karl Kautsky for example, but their most trenchant critics have been Marxists. So to assume that determinists correctly or mainly represent the Marxist tradition is like proclaiming that William Prynne is typical of all Puritans. For a longer account of these matters see J. Rees, *The Algebra of Revolution* (London, Routledge, 1998).

in circumstances of their own choosing' remark was that it was a recapitulation of his original methodological principles outlined as early as the *Theses on Feuerbach*. It was Marx's radically foundational statement of human agency, the conclusion of his critique of not one but two determinist and teleological systems, the materialist reductionism of Ludwig Feuerbach and the idealist teleology of Hegel.[2]

I

We can make these considerations a little more concrete by looking at some of the particularities of early-modern rebellions. Class analysis is often dealt with unsympathetically by historians of the seventeenth century but, even among those who reject a class framework for the analysis of political events, there is an acceptance that class is a relevant category when it comes to economic and social history. After all, class in this register is merely the relationship that a group of people have to the economic necessities of life: they are either landowners, or not; possess merchant capital, or not; employ others to work for them, or not. Contention over class does not usually arise from these widely accepted points. It begins at the point where these class distinctions interact with the social, political, and ideological spheres. In order to understand this interaction, we need to see the category of class in a much more expansive way than the critics, and sometimes the exponents, of class analysis allow.

Perhaps one of Marx and Engels' least appreciated but most important observations about revolutionary experiences before the rise of capitalism was that 'All previous historical movements were movements of minorities, or in the interests of minorities'. And Engels elaborated this thought, arguing that 'the common form of all these revolutions was that they were minority revolutions. Even where the majority took part, it did so - whether wittingly or not - only in the service of a minority; but because of this ... this minority acquired the appearance of being representative of the whole people.' Brian Manning simply observed, 'the vast mass of the people were neutrals.'

---

[2] M. Fulbrook, 'The English Revolution and the Revisionist Revolt', *Social History*, Vol.7, No.3 (Oct. 1982), p.261.

On this reading, John Morrill had no need to have the title of Reay and McGregor's *Popular Religion in the English Revolution* changed to *Radical Religion in the English Revolution* on the grounds that the subjects of the book 'were all profoundly unpopular groups'. 'Popular' in this context simply means non-elite rather than commanding a majority of the population's support. This is a matter of the first importance when it comes to evaluating claims made right across the early-modern political spectrum, from Monarchists, to Republicans, to Levellers, to speak for the 'common people of England'. Their ability to sustain such claims, which is not to say that the claims were even then true, rested on the outcome of political conflict, not pre-existing levels of approval in society at large. The second important peculiarity of the early-modern revolutions is that they were political revolutions not social revolutions. That is, they resulted in a transformation of the state machine, but not an immediate wholesale change in the structure of the economy, although longer-term change in ownership of economic assets was also a result of the revolution. The political revolution stemmed from, and further facilitated, economic change, but this was a much-extended transformation predating and postdating the revolution by many decades. Marx and Engels expressed this fact by saying that the new society develops 'in the interstices' of the old. And Christopher Hill wrote that, 'Such is the Marxist concept of bourgeois revolution, the revolution is overthrown by a middle class that has grown up inside it....'[3]

The consequence of this view is to reveal a more complicated class dynamic in these revolutions, at least compared to those occur-

---

[3] K. Marx and F. Engels, *The Communist Manifesto* (London, Verso, 1998), p.49. F. Engels, 'Introduction to The Class Struggles in France' (1895) in K. Marx, *The Class Struggles in France* (Chippendale NSW, Resistance Books, 2003), p.21. B. Manning, 'The Long Parliament and the English Revolution', *Past & Present*, No. 5 (May 1954), p.74. J. Morrill, 'Revisionism's Wounded Legacies', p.585. C. Hill, 'The English Civil War Interpreted by Marx and Engels', *Science and Society*, Vol.12. No.1 (Winter 1948), p.135. R. Brenner, *Merchants and Revolution* (Cambridge, CUP, 1993). G. Lukács, *History and Class Consciousness*, p.55.

ring after industrialisation. In the early-modern period, different members of one and the same class grouping may have very different relationship to the forces transforming the economic structure of the society. Two different landowners, indistinguishable in their general class characteristics, for instance, may nevertheless be significantly different in adopting market-oriented methods of cultivating the land, or not. Brian Manning long ago suggested that, in some areas, there might be 'a significant correlation between modernising landowners and the representatives of urban revolutionary cells' and in others, the south-west for instance, it would seem 'that old-fashioned landowners appeared more frequently on the Royalist side.' And even if a particular family of landowners are not themselves adopting new market-oriented methods of production, they may be politically, religiously, or ideologically drawn to causes espoused by others of the same class who are. The same point may be made about merchants. Alike economically, they may be monopolisers linked to the crown, or not. 'No historian would expect to find all the merchants on the Parliamentary side', remarked Brian Manning, 'especially as the Royalist merchants representing Bristol were monopolists.'

Robert Brenner's important contribution to the study of the English revolution was predicated precisely on investigating the distinctions between 'interloper merchants' and other more established merchant interests. Moreover, in pre-capitalist society, classes are never as distinct as economic formations as they become in full-blown capitalism. 'Hence the structuring of society into castes and estates means that economic elements are inextricably joined to political and religious factors.'[4]

This more expansive treatment requires that we see class in at least six related but distinct ways: as class location, class interest, class consciousness, class organisation, class political representation, and class conflict. Examining these distinctions more closely will give us a model of class which is neither reductionist nor teleological. We have already mentioned class in the sense that refers to the economic

[4] B. Manning, 'The Long Parliament and the English Revolution', pp.74-5. G. Lukács, *History and Class Consciousness*, p.55.

register: class location is an objective relationship to the means of production, such as 'landowner'. Of course, this will not exhaust the relationship between different groups and the land. That requires supplementary definitions: are we talking about large landowners or a peasant landowners? When we talk of wage labourers, do we mean those solely dependent on waged work, a day labourer, or the itinerant poor? Crucially, in the early-modern period, we have to follow contemporary commentators in distinguishing the middling sort, those who are in possession of some land or capital, and so not without social standing, from those who formed part of the ruling class nationally on the one hand, and the mass of wage workers, and the poor on the other.

By determining the class location of different groups, we can extrapolate their class interests, that is, what it is in the wider society which corresponds to the survival and prosperity of this group. Does this or that class have an interest in maintaining rights of land ownership, the ability to trade or produce profitably? Or do they have an interest in maintaining the rights of small landowners against big landlords? Do they have an interest in higher wages and lower prices? Or the reverse? Advocates of class analysis are sometimes accused of foisting their own prejudices onto social groups when they maintain that they have a class interest that might be different from their actually existing class consciousness. How, critics ask, can you simply attribute interests to a group that does not expressly articulate those same interests? This is a less secure argument than it might seem, for in everyday life we do this sort of thing all the time. 'George shouldn't smoke, it's bad for him', is a statement which is saying that, objectively, smoking is not in George's interest, irrespective of what George may say about the matter. What is true of individuals can also be true of political actors, including whole classes. Their ideology may or may not accurately reflect their class interests. Historians of all methodological persuasions routinely make such judgements, for instance, about Charles I. They rightly point to some of his decisions which are then argued not to have been in his personal interest, those of the royalist cause in general, or in the interests of the monarchy as an institution. In any given case, the argument may be right or wrong, but it is not wrong on methodological grounds.

Class consciousness does not have a direct, simple, or linear relationship with either class interest or class location. If it did, then we could simply read off the consciousness of classes from their location and the interests arising from them. But classes usually develop multiple conceptions of their own interests and their place in the wider society. Moreover, they are in a dynamic power relationship with other classes and this also shapes their own ideologies. Some classes have greater economic power than others and, deriving from this, a greater ability to shape ideology and consciousness, not only of their own class but of other classes as well. As a result of this fact, class consciousness is often an amalgam of a core of elements drawn from the class interests of a particular class, and other elements drawn from the ideology of other classes. Or to put it another way, class consciousness is shaped not only by class location and class interest but by the totality of class relations as they interact across the range of social experience.

Class organisation is often rooted in particular class experience but its programme and policy will be shaped by its interaction with other class forces, perhaps diluting, certainly influencing, the degree to which pure class interests are reflected in or attenuated by the organisational forms and programmatic demands of particular class organisation. Moreover, class organisation almost never reflects an economic class in its entirety. The Corporations of London did not represent all producers and merchants, and certainly not equally, just as modern trade unions do not represent the entirety of the working class. Even Conrad Russell's introductory chapter to *The Origins of the English Civil War*, as Mary Fulbrook points out, came close to substantiating this kind of analysis, even if he saw it as coincidental rather than conjunctural:

> The peculiar situation which produced the Civil War was the result of two coincidences. The first, in 1625, was the decision of the King to challenge the religious orthodoxy of the Parliamentary classes at the moment when the need to settle his finances had become desperate. The second, in 1640, was the alliance of discontent among the gentry with two separate social discontents, that of the poor and that of substantial merchants who were not part of this privi-

> leged group. Without these coincidences there would have been some form of political crisis during the century, but it would have been a very different crisis from the one which actually happened.[5]

Unfortunately, having correctly noted that the gentry did not react homogenously to the crisis of 1640-42, Russell does not develop his insight into the emergence of alliances between different classes and fractions of classes.[6]

Political organisation may be rooted in class organisation and reflected class interest, but it will also be a site where multiple class interests are reconciled or contained within a single political project. In addition, the personnel, particularly the leading personnel, of political organisations may not originate in the class which the political organisation represents. Gentry figures may represent merchant interests, merchants may speak for peasant interests. Representatives of the middling sort may articulate the views of those further down the social scale, such as debtors or commoners threatened by enclosure. Moreover, and typically, a single class may generate more than one political representative. Ruling classes may be represented in different ways by different political organisations or factions, which may have made their own political alliances with other classes. Political representatives of subordinate classes may represent one or more class grouping. Merchants and lower gentry may be represented by the same political current. Small masters, artisans, and poorer peasants may find their class interests and ideology reflected more or less accurately by the same political leaders.

Finally, none of this happens in a static situation. Conflict between classes, and the political and ideological formations which arise from them, repeatedly shape and reshape the possibilities open to those engaged in the political arena. Institutions, political groupings, and personalities that appear in one shape at a particular

---

[5] C. Russell quoted in M. Fulbrook, 'The English Revolution and the Revisionist Revolt', *Social History*, Vol.7, No.3 (Oct. 1982), p.257.

[6] M. Fulbrook, 'The English Revolution and the Revisionist Revolt', *Social History*, Vol.7, No.3 (Oct. 1982), p.257.

moment very often appear to have a quite different shape at another. How else should we see Denzil Holles' transformation from arch-critic of monarchy to promoter of a monarchical settlement? This is simply to recognise that historians are never investigating stable entities, timeless 'facts', but developing processes: 'Thus the knowledge that social facts are not objects but relations between men is intensified to the point where facts are wholly dissolved into processes', as George Lukács expressed it. And so, from this point of view, for instance, it is not an objection to Marx's analysis to say that the English Revolution opened with a revolt of the nobles.

Marx indeed made the point in his review of Guizot's history of the English revolution that both the English and the French revolutions began in this way: 'Guizot completely forgets that the French Revolution, equally conservative, began even more conservatively than the English. Absolutism, particularly as it finally appeared in France, was an innovation there too, and it was against this innovation that the parlements [French Diets] revolted to defend the old laws, the us et coutumes [usages and customs] of the old monarchy with its Estates General. And whereas the French Revolution was to revive the old Estates General that had quietly died since Henry IV and Louis XIV, the English Revolution, on the contrary, could show no comparable classical-conservative element.' But what only an analysis of the revolution as a dynamically conflictual process can explain is why a revolution that opened with a noble revolt ended in the abolition of the House of Lords and the execution of the chief aristocrat.[7]

II

This, admittedly, is a general schema. But it can be applied in productive ways to some of the discussions that have been raised about the socio-economic context of the English revolution. For instance, this framework allows us to say something useful about the dynamic

---

[7] G. Lukács, *History and Class Consciousness*, p.180. K. Marx, 'Review of Guizot's Book on the English Revolution', in *Surveys from Exile* (London, Penguin, 1973), p.252.

of local politics and national politics. The families that are examined in *The Fiery Spirits*, for instance, the Strodes in Devon, Alexander Rigby in Lancashire, Henry Marten in the Vale of the White Horse in Berkshire and Wiltshire all had relationships with their local constituencies. When Alan Everitt's pioneering work on Kent was published in 1966, it suggested that the county community was itself limited mostly to the ruling gentry, relatively closed to national influences, and predominately conservative politically. However, work since then, particularly by Clive Holmes and Ann Hughes, has reinvented county studies to include popular classes, powerful interactions of centre and locality, and indigenous as well as imported radical politics. These relationships are, as the account of the fiery spirits reinforces, sometimes complex, contradictory, and conflicted. It undermines the view of the county as 'an introverted, isolationist local unit', to use Clive Holmes' description.

William Strode and his father both certainly came to the Parliaments of the 1620s with concerns directly generated by social unrest in Devon. But their views were always hotly contested both locally and in parliament itself, and the local impulse seems to have weakened in the 1640s. If there was ever a 'national' politician it was surely Henry Marten, yet he had considerable popularity in his own locality as much because of, rather than in spite of, his radicalism. And though very focussed on national political developments, he was constantly engaged in affairs in his locality, not least militarily, since the front line between the Royalist capital in Oxford and Parliament's in London ran through his backyard, making the peaceful sounding names of Aylesbury and Abingdon, Wallingford, Reading, and Newbury into the outposts, garrisons, and battlefields of the civil war. Rigby's Lancashire base saw him adopt a strongly anti-papist stance in response to the heavily Catholic Royalism that confronted him. In this, he was at one with the county's Parliamentarians. Yet his own radicalism had to strike a fine balance with the heavily Presbyterian make-up of Parliamentarianism in the county. Ann Hughes' study led her to 'become sceptical about notions of a sharp contradiction between local and general concerns.' Indeed, it was never the case that these the county communities were completely sealed-off from national politics or unaffected by popular or radical political mobilisation. The dynamic certainly ran in both directions, sometimes national events overriding local developments, sometimes local events feeding into, or contradicting, national imperatives.[8]

Another relevant discussion was effectively framed by Clive Holmes in his review of Brian Manning's *The English People and the English Revolution*. Manning's thesis was that the middling sort in seventeenth-century England played a decisive role in the revolutionary events of the 1640s. Holmes' objection to Manning's thesis was that the middling sort did not just express their political aspirations through one political project, say that of the Levellers, but also through other, sometimes hostile and contradictory, projects. He gives as examples London peace petitioners, Clubmen, or London Presbyterians. Only 'a tiny minority of this group', Holmes concluded, espoused the Leveller demand for a 'greater measure of democracy'. Brunton and Pennington made a similar point in their classic study *Members of the Long Parliament*, where they concluded that their findings indicated 'some of the dangers in the general assertions which both Marxists and their opponents are apt to make'. In particular, Brunton and Pennington warned against the view that 'the war was the crisis of a class struggle' because of the 'absence of any marked difference between Royalists and Parliamentarians' in the House of Commons. 'On both sides', they concluded, 'there were merchants and lawyers; on both there were old landed families and new ones, families that prospered and families that failed.' In other words, Brunton and Pennington raise the same issue as Clive

---

[8] For an important overview of this debate see, J. Eales, 'Alan Everitt and The Community of Kent revisited', in J. Eales, and A. Hopper eds., *County Community in Seventeenth Century England and Wales* (Hatfield, University of Hertfordshire Press, 2012). Alan Everitt's original contribution is in *The Community of Kent and the Great Rebellion, 1640-60* (Leicester, Leicester University Press, 1966). Clive Holmes response to the debate is 'The county community in Stuart historiography' *Journal of British Studies*, Vol.19, No.2 (1980), pp.54-73. Ann Hughes ground-breaking study is *Politics, Society and Civil War in Warwickshire, 1620-1660* (Cambridge, CUP, 1987), p.xii. C. Hill, 'Parliament and People in Seventeenth-Century England: A Rejoinder', *Past & Present*, No.98 (Feb. 1983), pp.155-8.

Holmes: one social class, or more accurately in the case of both the middling sort and the gentry representatives in the Commons, one specific element of a social class, can sustain more than one political project.[9]

There are a number of important points to be discussed here. Firstly, Brunton and Pennington come to their conclusions by jumping register. They are making statements about whether class distinctions existed only among MPs within the House of Commons. If the focus were even a little wider, say including the Lords and the Court, that is the national governmental machine as a whole, we would have a rather different outcome. After all, in the end, most Lords did side with the King, and most MPs did not. As Brian Manning's rebarbative but nonetheless penetrating review of *Members of the Long Parliament* put it: 'The omission of the House of Lords is unfortunate because the typical Royalist was more likely to have been found there than in House of Commons. In an attempt to deny that the civil war was a clash between a "feudal aristocracy" and a "rising bourgeoisie" it is absurd to look for the feudal aristocrats in the Commons; and only slightly less absurd to look there for typical representatives of the rising bourgeoisie. But more important is the failure to study the relations between members and their constituencies.' Manning's concluding point is important: the social and economic struggles of the 1640s happened, as we would expect, across the whole face of the society and they did have an impact on MPs, even though the MPs themselves were a reasonably, though not completely, socially homogenous group. It is here we would need to look if we were to reach any broader conclusions about the way in which class conflict affected the formation of Royalist and Parliamentarian parties among MPs. Brian Manning, as Holmes generously pointed out, was particularly acute in showing how the Royalist 'party of order' emerged among MPs as a result of the upsurge of

[9] C. Holmes, 'Review of The English People and the English Revolution by Brian Manning', in *The American Historical Review*, Vol.82, No.1 (Feb. 1977), pp.96-7. D. Brunton and D. H. Pennington, *Members of the Long Parliament* (London, George Allen & Unwin, 1954), p.177. See also B. Manning and D. Pennington, 'The Long Parliament', *Past & Present*, No.6 (Nov. 1954), pp.85-91.

popular parliamentarianism in the early phases of the revolution. As Mary Fulbrook summarised this argument:

> …the very voicing of more radical demands from below, coupled with fears of counter-reforming moves from the King's side, forced a polarization of positions: with popular movements variously provoking either increasingly conservative fears for the King as the lesser of two evils, or increasingly radical programmes for reform in order to retain popular support. The winning of the City of London for the parliamentarian cause, and the wealth of the City of London (which cannot be divorced from analysis of the socio-economic developments of the previous century) were also crucial to the course of subsequent developments. Having rightly rejected simplistic forms of class analysis focusing solely on single classes in isolation and seeking (non-existent) coherent class intentions and actions, revisionists should not conclude that all forms of analysis of class relations, strengths and alliances should be declared beyond the bounds of explicit theoretical focus.[10]

Given the framework of different levels of class analysis that I have outlined, this outcome should be expected. A revolutionary crisis poses existential issues for all classes and fractions of classes. The reaction to this crisis in terms of consciousness, political movements, and political representation will always be multiform not unitary. This is why, even while politics is shaped by class formations, it can never be reduced to them in a linear manner. Social classes, or subsections of classes, like the middling sort or the gentry, will generate a variety of different political projects aimed at resolving the crisis in ways that are imagined to benefit them, and indeed the whole society. Which of these projects will become dominant is precisely what political conflict decides, and

[10] B. Manning, 'The Long Parliament and the English Revolution', pp.73-4. M. Fulbrook, 'The English Revolution and the Revisionist Revolt', pp.259-60.

those political conflicts inevitably draw on the wider social and economic resources that the various factions can mobilise. That is, the political conflict has its own logic, but that logic is shaped by, but not determined by, the wider economic and social resources available to the combatants.

From this perspective, the war and peace parties both embody a certain version of the class consciousness of the gentry, as do their successors, the Presbyterians and the Independents. Likewise, the middling sort can generate a peace project as well as a Leveller project, both of which embody a version of what outcomes might be convincingly said to represent the interests of those classes, or fractions of classes, from which they draw significant but not sole support. But, of course, not all convincing projects are equally viable, equally effectively expressed, or create equally effective political vehicles. Being initially convincing enough to generate some support does not guarantee victory in the arena of political struggle. That is a story that can only be told in the account of political struggle. The emergence of republicanism as a pivotal political project among Parliamentarians is one aspect of this process, primarily as a practical requirement imposed by the necessities of the struggle, an ideology emerging from the shell of an old order cracked open by revolution and civil war.

In the story of emerging parliamentary radicalism and republicanism, for instance, Royalist ideology is an important dimension. The notion that the revolutionary troubles in England in the seventeenth century were stirred up by a minority of fiery spirits had a long pedigree at court stretching back at least to James I. This was not a passing phrase or casual abuse of the monarchy's political opponents. It was a central prop of monarchist ideology. The essential thought was that the majority of subjects were content with royal government and that the peace of the nation was only being disturbed by a fiery or violent minority who were set on stirring up their otherwise happy neighbours. Such thoughts, blaming societal ills on a handful of malcontents, are now so well worn that it requires considerable historical imagination to see them as they were in the seventeenth century: relatively novel and, perhaps, more believable than the passage of time has rendered them today. Some such ideology is a necessary part of the self-justification of all states, and still plays an indispensable role today. The Crown's case in the contemporary Undercover Policing Inquiry, for instance, relies on the idea that political activity aimed at promoting the complete transformation of society is illegitimate and that the participation of individuals who hold such views in trade unions or protest movements is sedition. For every governing class must see itself as ruling over a society which is fundamentally as good as it can be. Gradual reform of this or that aspect of society might be desirable, but in essence the society must be the best imaginable. To agree to the alternative proposition, that a fundamentally different society would be better, is to declare ideological self-dissolution. People who believe this latter proposition must therefore be declared illegitimate at best, outlaws at worst.

In the seventeenth century, who exactly these incendiaries were, was an expandable category. They might be as few as a handful of named individuals or as great as whole social groups, say lawyers or sectaries, or all Puritans. In MP Sir Simonds D'Ewes' mind 'fiery spirits' was, as it had been for James I and was for Charles I, a portmanteau expression. The core of those for whom the term was used were certainly radicals, but there was a floating population of MPs who were also described as fiery spirits when they occasionally sided with the radicals or merely when they irritated D'Ewes. But on any and all definitions, Henry Marten, William Strode, Alexander Rigby, and Peter Wentworth were regarded as fiery spirits. In the context of this discussion, it is worthy of note that they were all from a gentry background, as were the overwhelming majority of MPs. The gentry were a minority of society, and the radical gentry representatives were a minority of their class, though they found allies in other parts of society. When the majority of their fellow MPs wanted to make a settlement with the King, and in this they represented a settled view of a considerable part of even the parliamentarians, it was this minority of a minority who grasped the political logic that reckoned that any such settlement would end in the defeat of the parliamentary cause in its totality. They became that section of the Commons, allied to that wider section of society, that was most determined to defeat the King and the entire royalist cause completely. Virtually no one who took their seat in the Long Parliament when it opened in 1640 imagined that they would end up declaring a Republic. And herein lies the importance of the relationship between class and politics. It is not the case that revolutionaries first made the revolution, but it is nevertheless true that the revolution made the revolutionaries. The Levellers became one part of that revolutionary camp, expressing a certain vision of the class experience of the middling sort. They became allied to another vital component of the revolutionary bloc, the fiery spirits, expressing a minority view among the gentry of how the revolution should be completed. In this, the political logic of events had exceeded the limits that the wider class structure of society could bear. The Protectorate and Restoration were the result of that fact.

III

Some additional clarity might be brought to this discussion if we looked at the contours of Marxism since its foundation. Its main phases have been, firstly, its elaboration by Marx and Engels and its development during their lifetimes. Secondly, its widespread adoption by international social democracy in the late Victorian era until the crisis of the First World War, and then by the Third International. Thirdly, the emergence of a Stalinised variant lasting, with declining appeal, from 1928 until 1989. Fourthly, a new radical Marxist revival that arose from the crisis of Stalinism in the 1950s and 1960s and the rebirth of student and industrial militancy in the West in the late 1960s and early 1970s. It is certainly true that some of the theorists associated with the institutionalised variants of Marxism, Karl Kautsky for instance, developed reductionist analyses. But it is equally true that their most trenchant critics were also Marxists, mostly those associated with the revolutionary wing of international social democracy before and during the First World War, notably Lenin, Trotsky, Luxemburg, Lukács and Gramsci. The rebirth of Marxism in the post-war period has been decisively anti-determinist, especially in its academic variants. Indeed, one of its most celebrated theorists, Louis Althusser, developed an entire methodology based on proving that 'the lonely hour of the "last instance" never comes', a riposte to Engels' own anti-reductionist formulation that economic relationships are only determinant in the last instance. But the main opposition to this structuralist Marxism, the so-called Hegelian Marxist tradition, was also radically, if more convincingly, opposed to reductionism.[11]

The main point to take from all this is that the broad Marxist tradition has been well aware of the issue of reductionism since its inception, and was indeed founded in opposition to one such current, the crude materialism of Ludwig Feuerbach. Moreover, Marxism is hardly the only methodology that produces reductionist patterns of thought. They are, particularly, repeated occurrences in empirical and positivist modes of thought as well. So, if we are to play whack-a-mole with reductionism, we will be playing it across a wide interdisciplinary lawn. But, entertaining as that might be, perhaps it would be more productive to see where the main exponents of Marxist interpretations of the English Revolution sit within this broad landscape of Marxism as a whole. Christopher Hill and Brian Manning are the most often cited exponents of a Marxist interpretation, but this ignores a wider contribution by other historians. Robert Brenner and Ellen Wood have both made substantial contributions to the debate about the transition from feudalism to capitalism and about the course of the English Revolution itself. James Holstun's *Ehud's Dagger* was a powerful re-examination of key aspects of the revolutionary process. Both Perry Anderson and Henry Heller have looked at the transformation of economic structure and class relations in the seventeenth century. Michael Sturza has recently contributed an overview of the role London played in the revolution. Norah Carlin has examined the crucial petitioning campaign of 1648-49. George Yerby has made a

---

[11] These broad contours of the development of Marxism are widely accepted both by Marxists like Perry Anderson in his *Considerations on Western Marxism* (London, Verso edition, 1979) and by informed critics of Marxism like Leszek Kolakowski in his three volume *Main Currents of Marxism* (Oxford, OUP, 1978). For another overview see J. Rees, *The Algebra of Revolution* and J. Larrain, *A Reconstruction of Historical Materialism* (London, Allen and Unwin, 1986). Althusser's formulation is in 'Contradiction and Overdetermination', *New Left Review* 41 (Jan/Feb 1967) in the section on 'Base and Superstructure'. See also C. Wickhan (ed) *Marxist History-writing for the Twenty-first Century* (Oxford, OUP, 2007), esp. Introduction.

serious reassertion of the economic drives that propelled England towards revolution. And Pepijn Brandon has written an outstanding analysis of the rise of the Dutch Republic in the seventeenth century.[12]

The issue here is not an appreciation of the breadth and depth of these contributions to the historiography of the seventeenth century, but to assess where these historians stand methodologically in relationship to debates on reductionism. For the purposes of this essay, we will look at the work of the best known of the Marxist historians: Hill, Manning, Brenner, and Wood.

In their early careers, both Hill and Manning were members of the Communist Party Historians' Group (CPHG), and this might be supposed to plant them firmly in a determinist intellectual tradition. But the CPHG was not a mere extension of the CP leadership or of Comintern intellectual orthodoxy as transmitted from Moscow, as Eric Hobsbawm's memoir of the group, compiled in discussion with Hill, makes clear. It was an unusually independent group of historians, 'virtually self-sufficient' in Hobsbawm's words, which followed its own paths of historical enquiry. One of the few foreign Marxist thinkers that impacted on the group was George Lukács, a key figure in the Marxist rejection of economic determinism. But, with or without that influence, Hobsbawm recorded that it was an 'advantage of our Marxism – we owe it largely to Hill and to the very marked interest of several of our members, not least A. L. Morton himself, in literature – was never to reduce history to a simple economic or "class interest" determinism, or to devalue politics and ideology.' The paper that Hill gave to the group on 'Ideas and literature,

---

[12] R. Brenner, *Merchants and Revolution* (Cambridge, CUP, 1993). E. M. Wood, *The Origin of Capitalism* (London, Verso, 2016), *The Pristine Culture of Capitalism* (London, Verso, 2015). P. Anderson, *Lineages of the Absolutist State*, H. Heller, *The Birth of Capitalism* (Halifax, NS, Fernwood, 2011). N. Carlin, *Regicide or Revolution? What Petitioners Wanted, September 1648-February 1649* (London, Breviary, 2020), G. Yerby, *The Economic Causes of the English Civil War* (London, Routledge, 2020). M. Sturza, *The London Revolution 1640-1643* (New York, Mad Duck, 2022), P. Brandon, *War, Capital, and the Dutch State* (1588-1795) (Chicago, Haymarket, 2016).

1660-1760' was, Hobsbawm recalls, 'particularly admired'. The continuing interest of the history from below school in plebian ideology is 'thanks largely to Hill' who made 'the social history of ideas … one of our main preoccupations'.[13]

Moreover, it was precisely in revolt against Stalinism that Hill and most of the CPHG left the Communist Party in the wake of the invasion of Hungary in 1956. 'The three most dramatic episodes of "opposition" – the Reasoner, the publication of a letter by a number of intellectuals in the New Statesman and Tribune, and the Minority Report on Party Democracy at the Twenty-fifth Congress of the CPGB, were all associated with communist historians (Saville, Thompson, Hilton, Hill, Hobsbawm, among others)'. After that, there was no impulse simply to take a determinist framework as given, and every reason to re-examine theoretical frameworks as part of a broader reassessment of political commitments. Hill may have become even more interested in the role of ideas in his later work, but this was a development of a powerful strand of his thinking that had always been present. Additionally, he had always been interested in the role of religion beginning with *The Economic Problems of the Church* and continuing through *The English Bible and the English Revolution*.[14]

The work of Robert Brenner and Ellen Wood took place in an explicitly anti-determinist methodological framework. Brenner and Wood were the founders and most well-known exponents of so-called 'political Marxism'. The term itself was coined by French

---

[13] E. Hobsbawm, 'The Historians' Group of the Communist Party' originally published in *Rebels and their Causes: Essays in Honour of A. L. Morton* (London, Lawrence and Wishart, 1978). The admiration for Hill's paper is recorded in footnote 17. The article is now available at https://www.versobooks.com/en-gb/blogs/news/the-historians-group-of-the-communist-party

[14] E. Hobsbawm, 'The Historians' Group of the Communist Party' originally published in *Rebels and their Causes: Essays in Honour of A. L. Morton* (London, Lawrence and Wishart, 1978) and now available at https://www.versobooks.com/en-gb/blogs/news/the-historians-group-of-the-communist-party. See also B. Manning, 'God, Hill, and Marx', *International Socialism*, No.59 (Summer 1993), pp.75-97.

Marxist historian Guy Bois during the 'Brenner Debate' on the transition from feudalism to capitalism in the 1970s. Bois described Brenner's approach as 'political Marxism' which he specifically distinguished 'economic Marxism'. The approach was said specifically to foreground political agency, class conflict, and historical specificity. In this, it was a counter to the refurbished orthodoxy of structuralist Marxism represented by Althusser and his followers. It was also an explicit response to what Wood described as the 'technological determinism' of G. A. Cohen's *Karl Marx's Theory of History: A Defence*. In defining her own stance, Wood wrote: 'The theoretical standpoint being proposed here is perhaps what has been called – disparagingly – "political Marxism". This brand of Marxism, according to a recent critic, is a "reaction to the wave of economist tendencies in contemporary historiography"'.[15]

Now, there's a deal to be said in criticism of this approach. In its foregrounding of class struggle, it could be read as diminishing the need to look at the social and economic limits of such struggles. And in its treatment of the preconditions of the capitalist mode of production, it might be said to dissolve a specifically economic dimension of the process into the social and political preconditions of the system. But what certainly could not be reasonably said of Brenner and Wood's approach is that it was any form of determinism, nor could it be realistically assimilated into broad brush accusations of reductionism. Such charges became even more untenable with the publication of Brenner's *Merchants and Revolution*. Again, there could be any number of arguments with Brenner's wider explanation of the role played by the group of 'new merchants' that he so brilliantly described and the wider explanation of the course of the English Revolution. Were the new merchants really quite as distinct from other merchants as Brenner suggested? Had he unduly privileged them as revolutionary actors compared with, in the early phases of the revolution, figures from the lower gentry and, in the

[15] T. H. Aston and C. H. E. Philpin (eds.), *The Brenner Debate* (Cambridge, CUP, 1985). E. M. Wood, 'The Separation of the Economic and the Political in Capitalism', *New Left Review* 127 (May-June 1981), pp.70, 72, 76. A. Callinicos, 'The Limits of "Political Marxism"', *New Left Review* 184 (Nov-Dec. 1990), pp.110-15.

later phases, middling-sort radicals? And where, throughout the revolution, did the actions of the London crowd sit in Brenner's overview of the revolution? But what could not be reasonably be said is that Brenner's account did not take account of political struggle or attempt to reduce it to any other economic or social register.[16]

It is noteworthy that in a serious and well-argued review of *Merchants and Revolution*, John Morrill did not make the criticism that Brenner was a determinist. Indeed, he noted that 'Brenner is insistent that the civil war was not inevitable' and conceded that 'he is quite right to criticize some revisionists in some of their writings for their "dismissal of any systematic social basis for seventeenth-century political conflicts".' On this issue, Morrill agreed that there was a social context for the revolution but denied that this meant there were social causes of the revolution. This seems to be a distinction without a difference, for if we cannot find anywhere in the social context, in however mediated a way, causes of the revolution, then why would historians even discuss context at all?[17]

Much as revisionism might have wished it, long-term causes and consequences cannot be avoided because the scale of change in the seventeenth century needs to be explained. Such explanations can be avoided in the microcosm of seminar papers but not in general accounts. One of the best of recent years, Jonathan Healey's *The Blazing World*, puts what changed over the seventeenth century in this way:

> 'By the end of the century, a new world had arisen. The great population rise had ended, but the economy kept growing: even labourers were earning more, and famine was now a thing of the past. There was a successful, if embryonic, welfare state. Towns were reborn as social hubs, rebuilt in brick and boasting coffee houses, theatres and concert halls. Trade was now the mainstay of economic life in a thriving market economy. Consumption was conspicuous and ram-

---

[16] R. Brenner, *Merchants and Revolution*. A. Callinicos, 'England's Transition to Capitalism', *New Left Review* 207 (Sept.-Oct. 1994), pp.124-33.
[17] J. Morrill, 'Conflict Probable or Inevitable?', *New Left Review* 207 (Sept.-Oct. 1994), pp.113-23.

> pant, while motive power was coming increasingly from coal. Plague was gone; executions were far less frequent; the witch trials were all but over; and you were much less likely to be prosecuted for illicit sex; English Protestantism had simultaneously become firmly established while also fragmenting into a world of Church and Chapel: not just the official Anglican establishment, but also the widespread – and accepted – existence of Dissent …
>
> The English monarchy – and its British successor – has never recovered the power it lost after this revolution … Indeed, the new state that arose out of this was recognisably ancestral to our own: regular Parliaments, the National Debt and the Bank of England and – of course – in 1707 the union between England and Scotland, all came soon afterwards.[18]

Healey's is a powerful description, but it requires an explanation of why this huge transformation took place. Healey is suspicious of explanations based on class, but it is hard not to see in his description the emergence of a recognisably bourgeois society where one did not previously exist. So what might a positive, non-determinist, Marxist account of the English Revolution look like? Brian Manning attempted to summarise his own view of events at the conclusion of the revolutionary crisis of the mid-seventeenth century in this way:

> 'I think that this is what was happening: the movements of some peasants and artisans in the 1640s were continuations of age old struggles against the exploitation and oppression of landlords and merchants, and shifted the revolution to the partial and temporary displacement of the ruling class from political power; but because of the extent of the growth of capitalism before 1640 this resulted, not in the victory of small producers, but in the acceleration of the development of capitalism. After the defeat of the monarchy, the peers and the church, the conflict in the 1650s between the forces for and against the development of capitalism was fought

---

[18] J. Healey, *The Blazing World* (London, Bloomsbury, 2023), pp.2-3.

> out within the Parliamentarian party and generated rapprochement between the rising members of the 'middling sort' and the old ruling class, that led to Restoration and the accelerated development of capitalism.'[19]

Manning has often been accused of over-reliance on the middling sort as the engine of revolutionary change. But here and elsewhere, his picture of the seventeenth-century crisis is much more complex. Indeed one of his most celebrated contributions is to have identified the way in which political struggle polarised in the early phase of the revolution and created both a Royalist party of order and a radical wing of parliamentarianism. This process is a pre-eminently political and ideological dynamic which, though it relates to a wider class structure, is not reducible to that class structure. To be precise, the same class structure would exist whether or not the political forces polarised in the way that they did in the period 1640-1642. That polarisation was an event largely explained by a political process of contestation.

In fact, Manning agrees with Hill that the driving force of the revolution was a class amalgam: 'the progressive smaller gentry, yeomen, free-trade bourgeoisie, supported by the masses of smaller peasants and artisans.' As Manning says, 'Hill uses the term "middling sort" for the same reason Barry Reay does, because he is not talking about a class but about "an amalgam of social groups stretching from the aspiring bourgeoisie to the lower-class elite…".' It is this conception of the class forces in the revolution that compels analysis in the direction of a necessarily irreducible role for politics. For what is necessary to bind the amalgamated class elements together is a shared political project both organisationally and ideologically. There are a variety of different expressions of this political necessity which represent either elements of this political bloc or the bloc as a whole. The London crowd was one loose but nevertheless organised expression of this political amalgam, stretching from the radical MPs to the artisans of the City. The Trained Bands provided another nodal point of organisation. The Independent and gathered churches performed this function for important elements in this

[19] B. Manning, 'God, Hill, and Marx', p.84.

broad parliamentarian front. So did the New Model Army when it was formed, as did the Levellers as they emerged as an organisation in the mid-1640s. Crucially, the parliamentarian radicals in the New Model, including its leading officers, the Levellers and the religious radicals formed an effective political bloc in 1648 to finally defeat the King. It is this process which I examined from the Levellers' point of view in *The Leveller Revolution* and from the radical parliamentarians' side in *The Fiery Spirits*.[20]

This thought, that different registers of a social totality, while they are related, each have their own modes of development which cannot be reduced to one another, is common enough in discussions of Marxist philosophy where it's known as a mediated totality. But it is virtually unknown among historians. It would perhaps be counter-productive to encourage too many historians to run into this thicket, but those that do wish to comment on Marxism and its supposed determinism might wish to at least acknowledge that many Marxists have profound methodological objections to determinism and that those Marxists historians who are best known for their work on the seventeenth century are among those who have long rejected reductionist formulations about the English Revolution.

---

[20] C. Hill, *God's Englishman* (London, 1970) quoted by B. Manning, 'God, Hill, and Marx', pp.78, 83. See also C. Hill, 'The Poor and the People in Seventeenth-Century England' in F. Krantz (ed.), *History From Below* (Oxford, Blackwell, 1988), pp.29-53. J. Rees, *The Leveller Revolution*. J. Rees, *The Fiery Spirits* (London, Verso, forthcoming 2025).

Chapter 3

The Levellers, the labouring classes, and the poor

The Levellers are best known as early advocates of an extended franchise and of religious and political liberties. They also claimed, and were understood by contemporaries, to be advocating social reforms that would improve the lot of the poor. William Larner, later a mainstay of the Leveller printing operation, was as early as 1641 producing material which wove together political demands and complaints about economic distress.[1] Bitter attacks on the wealthy and the powerful were a staple of Richard Overton's penmanship, but the quieter prose of William Walwyn was equally insistent on drawing attention to economic inequity and the plight of the poor. At least half of the thirteen demands that conclude Walwyn's *Gold Tried in the Fire* are of this kind.[2]

Yet the Levellers were equally clear that they rejected 'economic levelling' and historians have been quick to point out that they also were sometimes willing to qualify the widening of the franchise in important ways. This chapter seeks to show that this ambiguity in the Leveller programme was rooted in their social location and in the political allegiances that they chose to construct as a result.

It will further suggest that the paradoxes of the Leveller programme should not be read as dishonesty or incoherence, but as a necessary reaction to the social structure of seventeenth-century England. Leveller propaganda and programme embodied, sometimes consciously, sometimes instinctively in reaction to events, an attempt to construct a political alliance of sufficient breadth to have an impact on the development of the revolutionary crisis. I begin

---

[1] *To the Honourable House of Commons...* (London, 1641), Wing T1437.

[2] W. Walwyn, *Gold Tried in the Fire...* (London, 1647), E392[19]. See also W Walwyn, *Gold Tried by Fire* in J. R. McMichael and B. Taft, *The Writings of William Walwyn* (Athens and London, Georgia, 1989), pp.283-5.

with a sketch of some relevant features of the social and economic layer from which many Levellers came.

I

The immediate social circumstances in which the Levellers lived had a powerful impact on their conception of how society was, and should be, ordered. The Levellers were embedded, like most citizens, in a household economy. This was both a powerful economic reality and an equally influential ideological construct. Citizens were not atomised individuals going about their work or leisure in a society dominated by a free market either in labour or in commodities. The most common unit of production was not a large-scale workplace but the household, in both agriculture and urban manufacture.

Class location shaped Levellers' attitudes. The leaders of the Levellers were overwhelmingly from the middling sort.[3] They were, or had been, apprentices and became craftsmen, free of their respective City companies. John Lilburne, was famously apprenticed to the clothier Thomas Hewson. Thomas Prince, eventually co-treasurer of the Leveller movement, was also a clothier. Samuel Chidley, Prince's co-treasurer, was, like his father Daniel, free of the Company of Haberdashers. William Walwyn, older and more prosperous than most Leveller leaders, was from the Merchant Adventurers. William Larner, originally a Gloucestershire yeoman, was first apprenticed to the Merchant Taylors' Company. Edward Sexby was originally apprenticed as a grocer.

The head of household was not simply the dominant figure in the family, although this was also true, but the figure who determined the lives of servants and apprentices in the household. The head of household was automatically assumed to represent the whole household legally and politically. This is why there was no discussion of women being included in the franchise. The patriarchal structure of the fundamental economic and social unit of seventeenth-century society precluded such notions. Often when we use the term patriarchy today

---

[3] For an introduction to discussions around the middling sort see the relevant chapter in this book. See also B. Manning, *The English People and the English Revolution* (originally published in 1976, 2nd edition, London, Bookmarks, 1991), Ch.6.

it is simply as a synonym for 'women's oppression' or 'sexism'. But in seventeenth-century England, patriarchy was a much more all-encompassing social reality. And it included within it a relationship with the apprentices and the servants in the household as well as with female members of the family. For many, there was no such thing as 'going out to work'. Work was in the household, and the head of household was both head of the family and head of the business.

In such a society, it was difficult to imagine that either women, or servants, or wage labourers, dependent on others economically and socially, could exercise independent political agency. Later decades, indeed, centuries, would show that this was not an unfounded concern. Landlords and masters were fully capable of using their economic power to influence the way that their 'social inferiors' voted in elections.

Some of these figures, like Lilburne and Sexby, were from gentry families. But significantly, they were both second sons. As Earle observes, the spread of primogeniture meant that, as a study of Northamptonshire showed, 'by 1700, most younger sons of the county's gentry families had either gone into the church or into trade in London, while the daughters had married London merchants….' So, the term 'second son' was an acknowledged social category in mid-seventeenth-century England, carrying something of the meaning that 'angry young man' would carry in 1950s England. Second sons would not inherit, and therefore had to be apprenticed into trade. They were seen as a displaced and volatile social layer.[4]

The 'middling sort' would be thought of today as a smaller social category than those, however defined, working for wages. Wage earners are seen as a substantial, perhaps the largest single, category making up modern society.[5] In mid-seventeenth-century England, the social weight of these two elements was more or less reversed. One way of grasping this is to take a look at Gregory King's 1688

---

[4] G. E. Aylmer, 'Gentlemen Levellers?', *Past and Present* No.49 (Nov. 1970). P. Earle, *The Making of the English Middle Class* (London: Methuen Publishing Ltd, 1989), p.7.

[5] In proportions unchanged since 1983 the British Social Attitudes Survey finds that 60 percent of respondents identify as working class while 40 percent identify as middle class, see https://www.bsa.natcen.ac.uk/media/39094/bsa33_social-class_v5.pdf

table of social classes.

What is important in this context is the broad delineation of social groupings by a contemporary. From King we can see the wide variety of social layers that lie between the gentry and the labouring classes, all of whom might have been described as the middling sort. But what is also clear is that they are both numerically and in terms of economic, social, and cultural importance, a much more decisive sector of society than they are today. Those working for wages by contrast are much smaller and less important section of society than they are today. King's estimates show about 2.5 million people in the middle class and a similar number in the working class. This would make the middling sort in the seventeenth century in the order of twice the proportion of the modern middle class in contemporary society.

There has been some considerable debate about the accuracy of King's figures. One important investigation, by Peter Lindert and Jeffrey Williamson, suggests King actually underestimated the size of the middling sort and overestimated the size of the labouring classes.[6] Lindert and Williamson looked at 26 local censuses and burial records from 41 parishes in order to try and get a more accurate picture than King provided. The revised table of professions indicates that tradesmen and shopkeepers were more than double King's figure, while 'labouring people and outservants' were 80,000 fewer than King thought. The number of 'cottagers and paupers' were nearly 90,000 lower than King's figure. They concluded, 'numerous 17th century documents strongly suggest King grossly overestimated common labours and paupers, while undercounting artisans.' Moreover, the England revealed in Lindert and Williamson is, compared to King's picture, 'less agricultural and more industrial … the rich have got richer, the poor are fewer, and the middle groups more populated.' These conclusions are similar to those made by the new data of Cambridge University's Economies Past project and in Brian Manning's survey of the work of a wide range of historians, which estimated that wage labourers made up between one quarter and one third of the population.[7]

---

[6] P H Lindert and J G Williamson, 'Revising England's Social Tables 1688-1812', *Explorations in Economic History* 19 (1982), p.387.

[7] ibid. p.387, 392-394. B Manning, *The far left in the English revolution, 1640–1660* (London, Bookmarks, 1999) p.9.

Gregory King's estimate of population and wealth, England and Wales, 1688

Number of Families	Ranks, Degrees, Titles, and Qualifications	Heads per family	Numbers of persons	Yearly income per family
160	Temporal Lords	40	6,400	2,800
26	Spiritual Lords	20	520	1,300
800	Baronets	16	12,800	880
600	Knights	13	7,800	650
3,000	Esquires	10	30,000	450
12,000	Gentlemen	8	96,000	280
5,000	Persons in Offices	8	40,000	240
5,000	Persons in Offices	6	30,000	140
2,000	Merchants and Traders by Sea	8	16,000	400
8,000	Merchants and Traders by Sea*	6	48,000	200
10,000	Persons in the Law	7	70,000	140
2,000	Clergymen	6	12,000	60
8,000	Clergymen	5	40,000	45
40,000	Freeholders	7	280,000	84
140,000	Freeholders	5	700,000	50
150,000	Farmers	5	750,000	44
16,000	Persons in Science and Liberal Arts	5	80,000	60
40,000	Shopkeepers and Tradesmen	4½	180,000	45
60,000	Artisans and Handicrafts	4	240,000	40
5,000	Naval Officers	4	20,000	80
4,000	Military Officers	4	16,000	60
511,586		5½	2,675,520	67
50,000	Common Seamen	3	150,000	20
364,000	Labouring People and Out Servants	3½	1,275,000	15
400,000	Cottagers and Paupers	3½	1,300,000	6.5
35,000	Common Soldiers	2	70,000	14
849,000		3½	2,795,000	10.5
	Vagrants		30,000	
849,000		3½	2,825,000	10.5
511,586	Increasing the Wealth of the Kingdom	5½	2,675,520	67
849,000	Decreasing the Wealth of the Kingdom	3½	2,825,000	10.5
1,360,586			5,500,520	

Source: G E Barnett (ed), Two Tracts by Gregory King (Baltimore, John Hopkins Press, 1936)

TABLE 2
Revising the Social Table for England and Wales, 1688

	King (Barnet, *Two Tracts*)		Revised table	
Class	No. of families	Average family income (£)	No. of families	Average family income (£)
A. High titles and professions				
Temporal lords	160	2800	200	6060
Spiritual lords	26	1300	26	1300
Baronets	800	880	800	1500
Knights	600	650	600	800
Esquires	3,000	450	3,000	562.5
Gentlemen	12,000	280	15,000	280
Persons in offices, greater	5,000	240	5,000	240
Persons in offices, lesser	5,000	120	5,000	120
Persons in Law	10,000	140	8,062	154*
Clergymen, greater	2,000	60	2,000	72*
Clergymen, greater	8,000	45	10,000	50*
Persons in sciences and liberal arts	16,000	60	12,898	60
B. Commerce				
Merchants ... by the sea, greater	2,000	400	2,000	400
Merchants ... by the sea, lesser	8,000	200	8,000	200
Merchants on land, greater			3,264	400
Merchants on land, lesser			13,057	200
Shopkeepers and tradesmen	40,000	45	101,704	45
C. Industry and building				
Artisans and handicrafts	60,000	40	6,745	200
Manufacturing traders			162,863	38*
Building traders			73,018	25
Miners			14,240	15
D. Agriculture (excluding laborers)				
Freeholders, greater	40,000	84	27,568	91*
Freeholders, lesser	140,000	50	96,490	55*
Farmers	150,000	44	103,382	42.5*
E. Military and maritime (excluding traders)				
Naval officers	5,000	80	5,000	80
Military officers	4,000	60	4,000	60
Common seamen	50,000	20	50,000	20
Common soldiers	35,000	14	35,000	14
F. Labourers and the poor				
Labouring people and outservants	364,000	15	284,997	15
Cottagers and paupers	400,000	6.5	313,183	6.5
Vagrants	30,000	2	23,489	2
All Families	1,390,586	13.29*	1,390,586	39.18
Total pre-fise household income		£43,505,800		£54,440,248 (up 25.1%)

* King's own 1698 rivision (Holmes, 1977), pp67, 68.
* £32.17 after correcting for King's multiplication errors. Total population (King) 5.500,520
* £44,735,800 afrer correcting for King's multiplication errors in three classes (esquires, gentlemen, cottagers-paupers).

Source: P H Lindert and J G Williamson, 'Revising England's Social Tables 1688-1812', Explorations in Economic History 19, (1982), p393.

So, the conclusion that we might draw from all this is that the Levellers were part of an increasingly self-conscious and socially decisive group. Their ideas appealed to social groups below them, but these layers were less numerous than in modern society and were more socially marginalised than the middling sort to which the Levellers belonged.

The Levellers were of course not the only ones to appeal to the labouring classes and the poor. The Clubman movement was also an elemental expression of discontent among the same social group. And, as ever among subaltern classes, the political authorities could also rely on some support. After the revolution had established a republic, the Digger movement expressly raised the question of private property, making its abolition central to its programme.

These alternative expressions of discontent by wage labourers and the poor make an interesting comparison with the Levellers. The Clubmen were primarily a reaction to plunder, free-quarter, and taxation in the wartime conditions. They developed no political programme other than neutralism, although experience of treatment by Royalist and Parliamentarian forces sometimes led them to greater sympathy with the Parliamentarian cause. Deference and traditionalism are an inevitable part of any society, and it is no surprise that the crisis of the English Revolution inclined some to cling to the authorities they knew in the face of uncertainty and danger. The Diggers were neither as numerically significant as Clubmen nor Levellers. And they did not have the level of support for their programme nor the practical effectiveness of the Leveller movement. They were a small minority protesting in eloquent and incisive terms about the nature of the emerging Republic.

The Levellers' appeal to the poor and to the wage labourers was real enough. In what they had to say about equality before the law, abolishing monopolies, relief from debt, and the treatment of prisoners, they were genuinely raising issues of concern both to the middling sort and to those below them. Whether all these groups would benefit from the extended franchise was only part, if an important part, of what the Levellers had to say.

II

Perhaps the most famous discussion of the relationship between the Levellers and the labouring classes of the mid-seventeenth century comes in the Putney debates of 1647. These critical discussions between the most senior officers of the New Model Army, elected representatives from the army rank and file, and civilian Levellers have rightly fascinated historians.

One issue to which historical debate has frequently returned concerns whether or not the Leveller spokespeople at Putney advocated the expansion of the franchise implied in the *Agreement of the People*, first presented at Putney. Should it include the poorest males in society, or should servants and wage labourers be excluded from the vote?

It might be said that this issue has been over-analysed by historians. Jason Peacey, for instance, has suggested that historians have tended to divorce the study of a Levellers from the broader spectrum of radical Parliamentary opinion of which they were a part, and also that they have concentrated too narrowly on the franchise debate at Putney.[8] Both issues are of relevance here. The Levellers certainly were part of, indeed emerged from, a wider current of radical parliamentarianism. And the debate over the constitutional settlement of the nation after the First Civil War was actually one in which Levellers were engaged in debate with a much wider constituency of parliamentarians, some of whom contributed directly to the content of the *Agreement of the People*. Others held opinions with which the Levellers had to contend, even if they disagreed with them or distrusted those advancing them. We will see this dynamic at work throughout this discussion. But for all the differentiation

---

[8] J. Peacey, 'The People of the Agreements: the Levellers, Civil War Radicalism and Political Participation' in P. Baker and E. Vernon, (eds), *The Agreements of the People, the Levellers and the constitutional crisis of the English revolution.* (Basingstoke, Palgrave Macmillan, 2012), pp.76-96 See also M. Mendle (ed), *The Putney Debates of 1647* (Cambridge, CUP, 2001), P. Baker, 'The Franchise Debate Revisited: the Levellers and the Army', in S. Taylor and G. Tapsell (eds.), *The Nature of the English Revolution Revisited* (Woodbridge, Boydell and Brewer, 2013), Ch. 5.

among them, it is still the case that the Levellers were a distinct political movement. They recognised themselves as such, and their opponents did likewise.

Jason Peacey's second criticism is that discussion about the franchise debate is too narrowly focused. It is certainly true that the Levellers' reservations about the extension of the franchise are most easily seen in places other than the Putney debates. Especially since, for the most part, Leveller supporters at Putney are pretty clear that their proposals are meant to apply universally.

Thus, in perhaps the most famous statement of their case to come down to us from Putney, Colonel Thomas Rainsborough declared that 'the poorest hee that is in England' should have the same political rights as any other member of society, specifically the 'greatest he'. But this formulation was not new to Leveller thought. Both Elizabeth and John Lilburne had previously made precisely the same point in almost the same words. John Wildman, one of the Leveller representatives at Putney, also thought that 'every person in England hath as clere a right to elect his representative as the greatest person in England.' Edward Sexby thought that 'the poor and meaner of this kingdom' could not be denied the vote. Lieutenant Colonel John Rede spoke at Putney insisting that he could see 'noe reason why any man that is a native ought to be excluded.'[9]

The main axis of debate on both sides assumed that what is under discussion is a universal male franchise. Cromwell and Ireton objected to this proposal on the basis that if the poor are given the vote, they will use it to take property away from the rich. Rainsborough responded that unless the poor are given the vote 'I say the one parte shall make hewers of wood and drawers of water' of the rest and 'the greatest parte of the Nation bee enslav'd.' Sexby argued that though the soldiers had little property in the kingdom that they must be included in its political settlement.

Only on one occasion during the Putney debates does Leveller Maximillian Petty retreat from the idea of universal male suffrage. Petty suggested that servants or those dependent on others might be excluded from the franchise. This reads as a rather off-the-cuff response to debate with Henry Ireton, who has himself admitted

---

[9] J. Rees, *The Leveller Revolution*, pp.210-11.

that the franchise might be 'better than it is'. John Rede also adds an interesting cautionary note. He says that those who have given themselves over to 'voluntary servitude' should also be excluded from the vote.[10]

We can see a similar balance of opinion running throughout Leveller propaganda. There are frequent calls for the abolition of the Corporations and church tithes, both being seen as oppressive to the poor and all labourers. Equally frequently there are calls to relieve prisoners of debt.[11] The cause of the poor was espoused as: 'the too long continued shame of this Nation… of any to suffer such poverty as too beg their bread.' This condition should be 'forthwith effectually remedied: and to that purpose that the Poor be enabled to choose their Trustees, to discover all Stocks, Houses, Lands … which of right to belong to them ….'[12]

Nowhere is this approach more clearly displayed than in *The mournfull Cryes of many thousand poor tradesman, who are ready to famish through decay of Trade*, published in January 1648. The language was direct, and heavy with class antagonism:

> 'it's your Taxes, Customs, and Excise, that compells the Countrey to raise the price of food, and to buy nothing from us but meer absolute necessities; and then you of the City that buy our Work, must have your Tables furnished, and your Cups overflow; and therefore will give us little or nothing for our Work, even what you please, because you

---

[10] ibid. pp.210-12

[11] The petition of March 1647, in Wolfe, pp.139-40. The petition of January 1648, in Wolfe, p. 268. Petition of September 1648, in D. Wolfe, *Leveller Manifestoes of the Puritan Revolution* (Frank Cass, 1967), p.288. And one Leveller at least, James Freize, was a consistent advocate of prison reform. See R. Bell, 'Dens of Tyranny and Oppression: the Politics of Imprisonment in Seventeenth-Century London' (PhD dissertation, Stanford University, 2017), see especially pp.343-69. I grateful to Richard Bell for sending me his work. On Freize's Leveller affiliation see J. Freize, *The Levellers Vindication…* (London, 1649). E573[8].

[12] 'The petition of January 1648', in D. Wolfe, *Leveller Manifestoes of the Puritan Revolution* (Frank Cass, 1967), p.270.

> know we must sell for moneys to set our Families on work, or else we famish: Thus our Flesh is that whereupon you Rich men live, and wherewith you deck and adorn yourselves.'[13]

Popular petitions which supported the Levellers' key demands struck the same note. The petitioners who wrote *A Declaration of the Wel-Affected in the County of Buckinghamshire* assailed the 'extorting Lords of Mannors, Monopolists, Incroachers, Inhancers and other interested parties,' who act as 'great obstructors and hinderers of all our Liberties, Freedoms, and naturall Rights', and goes on to attack the 'arbitrary nature of Customs, Tolls, Monopolies,' 'wicked Customs, as Fines, Hariots, Quit-rents, and Headsilvers, with all slavish and base Tenours, Tyths, Impropriations, and Patents, Prerogative Charters' that violated the 'Liberties, Freedoms, and naturall Rights' of the commons. They argued that this was 'the originall of all our slavery, both in Tenure, Termes, tyrannical Laws, Customs, &c. whereby we, the lower sort of People, are made slaves to the wills of Tyrants, by reason the Law, being an outlandish Tongue, and withall bought and sold by the lawyers, who judge the Causes according to the Purse, and will do no Justice without money; so for filthy lucre, will stand to justifie and maintain any unjust, and wicked, and tyranicall Custome, or illegal persecutions of any Tyrants whatsoever; although to the utter deprivation and undoing of the poor widows, fatherless, & to the advancing the Wills of merciless Tyrants.'[14]

The Levellers' Large Petition of 11 September 1648, the most extensive programmatic collective document the movement produced, the *Agreement of the People* notwithstanding, contained a raft

---

[13] *The mournfull Cryes of many thousand poor tradesman, who are ready to famish through decay of Trade* in D Wolfe, *Leveller Manifestoes of the Puritan Revolution* (Frank Cass, 1967), pp.275-6.

[14] See G Kennedy, *Freemen, Free Labor, and Republican Discourses of Liberty in Early Modern England*, available at https://www.academia.edu/1828606/Freemen_Free_Labour_and_Republican_Discourses_of_Liberty_in_Early_Modern_England?auto=download. See also, for instance, the programmatic *New Engagement, or, Manifesto* of 1648 (noted as collected August 3rd), p.669.

of social reforms. The Levellers' enemies were quick to point this out. In a substantial pamphlet produced to refute the Large Petition, we read that the social demands are those of 'absolute Levellers' who are 'labouring to make Kings, Queens, Princes, Earles, and Lords with themselves as fellows at football, and equall to the poorest Peasant … they desire … that all Excise may-be abolished, and that all inclosures of Fens, and other Commons should be laid open, or inclosed onely and chiefly, to the benefit of the poore, whose Patrimonie they are.' In the wave of popular petitioning that followed the Large Petition, at a time when purely political demands might predominate, Norah Carlin has found that 'many subsequent petitions show knowledge of and support for these reforms, and half a dozen include a selection, or their own similar proposals'.[15]

This then was the dominant tone of Leveller rhetoric. But amidst this, the second strand of argumentation, just audible at Putney, also persisted. There were clear denials that economic levelling of any kind was part of the programme, and in the second edition of the *Agreement of the People*, it was explicitly stated that electors would not include servants or those 'receiving wages from any particular person'.[16] This exclusion also appears in the *Agreement of the People* of December 1648. Also excluded were those who had aided the King or who were not willing to sign the *Agreement*.[17]

So how should we understand this ambiguity in Leveller politics? At one level, we can understand Leveller reservations about the inclusion of servants and wage labourers, and indeed royalist sympathisers, as a response to immediate political pressures.

At Putney, the Levellers were in debate with the most senior officers in the army who also happened to be leaders of the Independents. They were under some considerable pressure to modify the

---

[15] *A Full Answer to the Levellers Petition* (19 September 1648), Wing F2343. The Large Petition of 11 September 1648 is *The Humble Petition of divers well-affected Persons* (London, 1668), E464[5]. N. Carlin, *Regicide or Revolution?*, p.9.

[16] The petition of January 1648, in Wolfe, p.270. *The Agreement of the People*, in D Wolfe, *Leveller Manifestoes of the Puritan Revolution*, p.297.

[17] *Foundations of Freedom: or an Agreement of the People*, in D Wolfe, *Leveller Manifestoes of the Puritan Revolution*, see pp.291, 342.

Agreement of the People in ways acceptable to the Independents. The subsequent two editions of the *Agreement of the People* were produced when cooperation between the Levellers and the Independents was at its peak. It is certainly possible that the Levellers were attempting to produce a document that would gain the support of Cromwell, Ireton, and their co-thinkers.

They may well have been encouraged to think that this was a compromise worth making because servants and wage labourers, dependent on their masters in a way that the middling sort of craftsman were not, were seen as not fully capable of exercising their vote independently. And so, as with the supporters of the King, it might be unwise to include them in the franchise least they pose a threat to a political settlement aimed at by the radical leadership of the Parliamentary cause, Leveller and Independent alike.

Ultimately, of course, the Cromwellians decided that a republic without any form of democratic consent was necessary, but at this earlier stage, we can see that Levellers too had to reckon with the possibility that too wide a franchise would open the door to counter-revolution.

This political paradox was real enough. But it rested on the deeper economic differentiation among supporters, or potential supporters, of the Leveller movement discussed earlier.

III

Let's look at how this relationship between Leveller demands and social layers beneath the middling sort worked in the dynamic process of revolution. Several complex issues are involved here. For instance, although class location, political consciousness, and political programme are related, they are not always related in simple and direct ways. So, although it is possible to see the way in which the social position of the Levellers was reflected in their political programme, it is also the case that others from very similar social backgrounds adhered to other political programmes. Similarly, as we have seen, the poor and wage workers might be attracted to the Clubman movement, popular Royalism, the Levellers, or the Diggers. Or, to more than one of these at different stages of the revolution.

What this should tell us is not that analysis of economic location is irrelevant but that alone it is not a sufficient explanation of political allegiance. For that, an additional analysis of politics is required, specifically the competitive process of constructing political loyalty and the dynamic of the social process in which this takes place.

Marx and Engels provided a specific account of these determinants for the pre-capitalist revolutionary experience. They maintained that the English and French revolutions were made by 'minorities, or in the interests of minorities'. In other words, while their expectation was that the revolutionary subject in modern society, the working class, was a majority and could be seen as speaking for a majority, this was not the case for the revolutionary movements which preceded the full establishment of capitalism. But if previous revolutionary movements were the movements of minorities, this immediately raises the question of what the relationship was between the revolutionary minority and broader sections of society who might or might not be engaged in the struggle with the old order.[18]

Marx and Engels argued that to engage such decisive wider forces, the assault on the old order had to be carried out under universalist demands which, though they resulted in the triumph of a minority, still held meaning for the plebeian forces mobilised in the conflict. As Engels put it, '… although, on the whole, the burghers in their struggle with the nobility could claim to represent at the same time the interests of the different working classes of that period, in every great bourgeois movement there were independent outbursts of that class which was the more or less developed forerunner of the modern proletariat … in the great English Revolution, the Levellers; in the great French Revolution, Babeuf.'[19]

Even in the French Revolution, Engels thought the bourgeoisie was too timid to carry through its own revolution and that 'the plebs had to do all the work'. This would not have happened unless the 'plebeians hadn't read a meaning into the revolutionary demands of the bourgeoisie they didn't have, if they hadn't pushed equality and

---

[18] H. Draper, *Karl Marx's Theory of Revolution, Vol. II, The Politics of Social Classes* (New York and London, Monthly Review, 1978), Chs.7, 10.

[19] F. Engels, *Anti-Duhring* (Peking, Foreign Languages Press, 1976), pp.20-1.

fraternity to extreme conclusions turning the bourgeois meaning of these catchwords on its head.'[20]

Marx and Engels were careful, as Christopher Hill long ago noted, not to overstate the degree of working-class development: 'In both revolutions [the English and the French] the bourgeoisie was the class which found itself effectively at the head of the movement. The proletarians and those fractions of the burgher class that did not belong to the bourgeoisie either still had no interests separate from the bourgeoisie or still did not form independent evolved classes or sub-classes.'[21] Nevertheless, the necessary 'excess of revolutionary activity' imparted to the movement by the mobilisation of the lower orders is one element that makes victory possible: '... as always - irony of history - this *plebeian* conception of the revolutionary catchwords became the mightiest lever for accomplishing this opposite: bourgeois equality - before the law, and fraternity - in exploitation.'[22]

Once the victory against the old order has been obtained, the social bloc between the middling sort, the labouring classes, and the poor is bound to break apart. Then a reverse dynamic takes over: 'It is the fate of all revolutions that this union of different classes, which in some degree is always the necessary condition of any revolution, cannot subsist long. No sooner is the victory gained against the common enemy than the victors become divided among themselves into different camps, and turn their weapons against each other.'[23]

We can see this dynamic at work in the relationship between the Independents and the Levellers, and between the Levellers and wage labourers and the poor. The social location of the Levellers is clear. They were the middling sort of craftsman and apprentices. They were not court monopolists, and not at the top of livery companies

---

20 F. Engels, Letter to Kautsky, 20 February 1889, https://www.marxists.org/archive/marx/works/1889/letters/89_02_20.htm
See also H. Draper, *Karl Marx's Theory of Revolution*, Vol. II, pp.273-5.

21 K. Marx and F. Engels, quoted in C. Hill, 'The English Civil War Interpreted by Marx and Engels', p.145.

22 F. Engels, Letter to Kautsky, 20 February 1889.

23 F. Engels [and K. Marx], *Revolution and Counter-Revolution in Germany* (London, Lawrence and Wishart, 1933), p.41.

and, therefore, of City government. Nor were they, with the exception of Henry Marten, leaders in parliament or, with the exception of Thomas Rainsborough, in the armed forces of parliament. But neither were they poor, or wage workers. Their programme reflected this: political and religious freedom of expression, equality before the law, democratic accountability ... but also free markets, the right to property, no economic levelling. But that was not the end of the matter. Leveller rhetoric did speak of the poor and their plight. They were not acting or speaking dishonestly in this matter. Political democracy must be universalist, and the long-term impact of raising this issue, even when programmes of the day did not fully embody it, was bound to enlarge the political possibilities of the poor as well as of the middling sort.

Nor can demands for democracy wholly ignore its economic impact: the poor may use their vote against the rich, as Cromwell feared. Ireton argued against Rainsborough at Putney because he had 'an eye to property'. The Levellers may have actually refused to countenance 'economic levelling', but on many occasions, if not always, their advocacy of the political rights of the poor was bound to embolden those who did wish to use political power for the purposes of advancing an egalitarian economic programme. And many Leveller social demands raised the condition of the poor quite independently of the relationship to the franchise. And so, even though the poor would find new masters in the new world, their political horizons had been enlarged.

Chapter 4

The middling sort

The middling sort is a term much used in the seventeenth century and much used by contemporary historians. It was and remains a controversial category, partly because of some inherent difficulties in defining exactly who the middling sort were, but more so because of the contested issue of how important they were in determining the course of events in the 1640s.

The difficulties of definition stem from the fact that any sociological group that stands between two others will shade into both the class above them and the class below them. Even today, when socio-economic classes are perhaps more distinct than they were in the seventeenth century, political scientists find precision difficult in the intermediate zones where the middle class fade into the ruling class over them or the working class below them. Nevertheless, the term middling sort is used so widely and regularly in the seventeenth century that is clear that contemporaries were very certain that an identifiable core phenomenon existed, even though they, like historians, might have difficulties in deciding exactly who was one side or the other of the borderline.

I

The reason why those in the seventeenth century talk so much about the middling sort is that they were a very large proportion of the population, much larger than the modern middle class. For this reason they included a very wide spectrum of actual professions and they were differentiated by whether they were in town or country. What they all had in common was that they were small producers not dependent on selling their wage labour. In a still predominantly agricultural economy, they were peasant farmers, and in industry, they were handicraftsmen and artisans. As Brian Manning noted, 'They were independent small producers in that, and so long as, they did not work for wages but were self-employed, and that, and so long as, they had property and were in possession of the means of production.'[1]

This class was both growing and differentiating in the seventeenth century. It was growing because the numbers employed in manufacture were growing at the expense of agriculture. It was differentiating because, as the capitalist market penetrated both agricultural production, trade, and urban manufacture, some of the middling sort were accumulating capital and rising into the ruling class and others were losing out and becoming wholly or increasingly dependent on wage labour. Embourgeoisfication and proletarianisation were eating away at the middling sort from opposite ends of the economic spectrum.

The account of the growth of the numbers involved in manufacturing and the decline in those in agriculture has recently been strongly re-enforced by the data released by the Economies Past project at Cambridge University. This two-decades long research has resulted in 'most detailed quantitative picture of long-run economic development ever assembled anywhere in the world.' The data show that in the period between 1600 and the Restoration of the monarchy in 1660, the economy underwent one of the steepest falls in agricultural employment and sharpest rises in manufacturing employment ever. The percentage of men employed in agriculture fell from 65 to nearly 45 percent. The percentage of men employed in manufacturing grew from 28 to over 40 percent. These changes are faster than during the industrial revolution itself. They, by and large, preceded the existence of large-scale machinery, factory development, and urbanisation. These changes were reflected in the social standing of the middling sort. There is a never-bettered description of what this looked like in Peter Earle's under-valued *The Making if the English Middle Class*.[2]

Earle's dissection of the London middle class starts 28 years before the final settlement of the English Revolution in 1688, but

---

[1] B. Manning, *Aristocrats, Plebeians and Revolution in England, 1640-1660* (London, Pluto, 1996), p.8.

[2] See https://www.economiespast.org/ (accessed 9 April 2024). P. Earle, *The Making of the English Middle Class.*

much of what he says describes processes that had been at work over the whole century. He describes a society in which bourgeois methods of business and government are already well advanced. By looking in detail at wills, probate records, household and business accounts, Earle has collated a detailed picture of the middling sort. In the course of his account, Earle deals some heavy blows to the most cherished myths of the revisionist historians. Take, for instance, the common argument that country communities, whether we talk of the middling sort or the lesser gentry, were sunk in rural seclusion with little interest in events in the capital and that, if they fought in the revolution at all, it was over local rivalries which had little in common with the economic or political conflicts of the metropolis. Earle, however, finds very close connections between the middling sort of London and their country cousins. The spread of primogeniture meant that the eldest sons inherited the land, but the younger sons were increasingly sent into trade or the professions:

> 'Since the best place to do this was London, an intricate web of relationships was woven between the middling people of London and the county and the country gentlemen. A study of Northamptonshire shows that, by 1700, most younger sons of the county's gentry families had gone either into church or into trade in London, while the daughters had married London merchants much more frequently than the sons of local gentry families.'[3]

We know, not least from the social profile of leading Levellers, that this was a trend well developed before 1640.

This 'trade' was not simply merchandising, it involved *production* on a capitalist basis. Earle rightly starts his analysis of London with manufacturing, 'a facet of the metropolitan economy often overlooked by historians, despite the fact that London was the greatest manufacturing city in Europe and was at the peak as an industrial centre relative to the rest of the country.' Earle quotes one study based on a sample of burial registers which estimates that some 60 percent of the occupied labour force were engaged in production,

---

[3] P. Earle, *The Making of the English Middle Class*, p.7.

although he himself estimates a lower figure of 40 percent. Even the lower figure is still 'higher than commerce or services, the two types of occupation normally stressed.'

Earle looks at the textile industry employing 40,000 to 50,000 people, perhaps 20 percent of the workforce, and sometimes using complex equipment like the knitting frame of which there were 500 in London in 1600 and 2,500 by the early 1700s. The metalworking and leather industries were the next biggest, each employing 10,000 people. The building trade, London's 36 shipyards, a food and drink industry of substantial proportions, all added to this manufacturing core of the city.

In all these industries, an increasing division of labour was quickly eating away at the old artisanal and guild methods of production and replacing them with capital-wage labour relations. Although the majority of workplaces were run by a master who oversaw apprentices and journeyman, Earle warns against the 'superficial continuity' this appears to show with feudal forms of production. He says it was 'increasingly difficult for journeyman to become masters, with the result that the numbers of permanent journeymen … were rapidly increasing.' In short, these frustrated journeymen were becoming wage labourers.

The small masters themselves were victims of capitalist accumulation as well, so that 'nearly every branch of London industry required a greater capital to run it as time went on … small masters … tended more and more to sell to big masters or to specialist shopkeepers and wholesalers, rather than to the public.' These retailers could easily move in on their suppliers making them into 'mere wage-earners or piece workers as economic power tended to move away from the maker to the seller.'

This process was furthest advanced in industries like cloth production, which required the use of machines. The big masters could often make economies of scale, say in the buying of raw materials, and were able to undercut their smaller competitors 'and to reinforce the trend towards the concentration of ownership of machines into fewer hands'. But 'the development of workshops in which large numbers of journeymen worked together did not require the invention of machines or other innovations, since these "proto-factories" had their own economic logic.' This logic resulted in less waste, closer supervision and economies of scale. Earle concludes,

> 'What one is seeing then is an increase in the scale of operation of the wealthier masters sometimes in the form of bigger workshops, sometimes to the extension of the "putting-out" system and sometimes through the use of their economic power in the market.'[4]

Some Marxists have argued that merchants were separate from this development in manufacturing, that they made their profit from buying at a low price, often overseas, and selling at a higher price. They were not, it is argued, interested in accumulating capital by exploiting wage labour. From this, it is argued that they had little interest in challenging the old feudal or absolutist order.

Earle makes it clear that this distinction between merchant and manufacturing capital has to be treated with great care. Some of the richest merchants certainly did have fortunes and social standing the equal of many aristocrats but, says Earle, 'the typical merchant was not the plutocrat he is sometimes taken for. The fortunes of the richer manufacturers came into the same range.' Neither were the economic roots of this wealth distinct, since 'some merchants had domestic interests in wholesaling, manufacturing or property.' In fact, domestic merchants were closely linked to production. It was said of one group of London cloth merchants that they were 'originally but the servant of the maker, but is now become his master, and not only his, but the wool merchant's and draper's too.'

But perhaps, as some historians argue, these merchants and manufacturers were simply absorbed by the aristocracy once they became rich. Certainly some contemporaries thought that the rich merchants and manufacturers soon returned to the country and bought their own mansions. One witness of the 1690s says, 'No sooner do they acquire wealth, but they quit traffick and turn country gentlemen.' This, however, was true only of a conspicuous minority. Earle's sample of the rich merchants shows only 25 percent owned real estate. He concludes that the acquisition of large real estate was not an all-consuming passion for the business community. Earle finds

---

[4] ibid. p.29.

that, in his sample, the value of real estate came below that of loans, mortgages, and company stocks and bonds. This is not surprising since, as Lord Hervey put it in 1707, 'How much better money yields than land, which after taxes and repairs allowed never answers above 3 percent.' Earle contrasts this with Richard Grassby's calculation that average profits for the period after 1650 were between six and twelve percent, but could range much higher in certain trades.[5]

Even the estates which do feature in the inventories that Earle examines are not necessarily evidence of merchants and manufacturers buying into the aristocracy. Often, they were inherited from the merchant's or his wife's family. In other words, they point to a move away from the land, not a return to it.

Small wonder that in the years that followed the revolution, there was an unprecedented expansion of the Stock Exchange, joint-stock companies, banking, insurance, and indeed the Bank of England itself. And alongside this booming capitalist economy arose a blooming bourgeois society. The professions, employing perhaps one third of the London middle class, mushroomed at the expense of the gentry whose sons became lawyers, teachers, churchmen, army or Navy officers, and state employees.

Unsurprisingly, an increasingly bourgeois culture attended to the needs of this rising class. The arts were less dependent on noble sponsors and court patronage. Instead, they were well on their way to becoming businesses just like those that gave their audience the money to be able to enjoy the performance. This was even true of the theatre, although it was one of the arts least patronised by the middle classes because 'so many of the plays performed on the Restoration stage were designed to mock the pretensions of the cits [citizens] and to insult the honour and taste of their wives.' Yet the theatre 'offered scope to the entrepreneur, most theatre buildings being built and owned by investors who received an income of so much per acting day from theatrical companies.' The Restoration, often offered as proof of the continued aristocratic dominance, is actually proof of the exact opposite. The Restoration comedies might parade the aristocracy's supposed superior manners, but even in this chosen arena, the bourgeoisie were surrounding them. In fact the public play itself

---

[5] ibid., pp.153-5.

was a form that fitted the needs of bourgeois society. The aristocracy's preferred form of drama, the court masque, performed for and flattering to the Lord or monarch's small private coterie, was now being superseded by plays performed before a paying public.[6]

Another modern institution was also being born around this time - the school. London was famous for its schools and 'the high level of literacy in the capital in all classes and both sexes suggest that elementary education was widely available and reasonably competent.' The money for the schools came from the middle-class pockets and was 'just enough to create a dutiful and subordinate working class', and to 'turn the children of the poor from pagan savages into obedient and Christian apprentices and servants'. The content of education was changing as well. In particular, the middle classes were 'losing faith in the educational value of the classics since, as one contemporary put it, "the learning of grammar schools is of little or no use to such as are set to ordinary trades".' The battle of the moderns against the classics, of the scientific revolution against the ancient Greeks, a struggle which had numbered Milton in its vanguard in the middle of the seventeenth century, was now a matter of practicalities for a generation enjoying the fruits of the victory of the English revolution.[7]

In short, every corner of this society was being rapidly, by the previous if not by later standards, transformed. It is the great virtue of Earle's eye for detail that he captures so many of these facets. Take, for example, street lighting:

> 'The old system required householders to display lanterns with candles lit from dusk to nine o'clock on moonless nights during the winter; as one can imagine, it was a fairly ineffective system ... However the 1680s saw the development of street lighting companies which contracted with individual householders to take over their lantern responsibilities for an annual payment. The company used oil burning lamps incorporating mirrors and bulls-eye lenses to intensify the light, an improvement which was sufficient to

---

[6] ibid. p.59.
[7] ibid. p.65.

> encourage a much greater public use of the evenings, as theatres opened and closed later and more people went on to taverns and coffee houses afterwards. The new system was gradually extended and improved, so that by 1736 the City was lit from sunset to sunrise throughout the year, making it the best lit urban area in the world.'[8]

This is the kind of social history at which Earle excels. It allows one to see the social revolution that had been made possible by the civil war seeping into every conceivable pore of society. There are however a number of qualifications that need to be made about Earle's account. He limits himself to a discussion of London, and London was certainly the most advanced part of the country and as such it showed the rest of the country its future. But, for these very reasons, it is atypical. It would have been a great advantage if Earle had followed his merchants and manufacturers out into the country, to their suppliers, down the arteries of the putting-out system, to see how their methods and ideas related to the rest of the country.

A greater weakness is that while this book is about class, but not about class struggle. It is not that Earle unsympathetic to Marxism. He says,

> '...the social structure of our period look[s] specifically like that of Victorian times as described by Karl Marx, a fact which should not be surprising since Marx's society grew out of the one discussed in this book. Marx analysed society on economic lines and writers in our period were beginning to do the same, moving away from the conservative view of the world in which status, esteem and degree were the criteria for ranking the social order. Such changes in description were necessary to take account of the changes in society brought about by the economic development from the 16th century onwards ... the social polarisation which accompanied these changes had created increasing numbers at the bottom of society who were completely divorced from ownership or the use of land or any other form of capital ...

---

8 ibid. p.78.

> Such, in embryo, were the proletariat who were later to be described by Marx.[9]

He notes that, although 'very few' of middling sort were like the capitalists that Marx analysed,

> 'What lifted them out of the mechanick part of mankind was the fact that their activities not only fed and clothed them but also enabled them to accumulate on a regular basis and so improve themselves. It was, then, accumulation and improvement, as well as the employment of capital and labour, which would be essential features of the middle sort of people.'[10]

Yet this excellent framework for looking at the development of bourgeois society remains underutilised. Earle provides simple, clear, scholarly research that restates in new depth some elementary truths about the nature of the society that issued from the English revolution and it makes the case that a rising bourgeoisie is a vital aspect of seventeenth-century history. But it analyses the middle class from the inside, not in their relations with other classes. In this sense it would be wrong, despite the similarity of their titles, to see this book as a counterpart to E.P. Thompson's *The Making of the English Working Class*. Thompson's book stressed that class identity is forged not just by economic circumstance but also by economic and political struggles with other classes. Earle's book omits this dimension almost entirely. The political struggles of the period, the echoes from the civil war, received barely a mention. This is an analytical account, not a dialectical account. It is interested in the facts about how things were, not in the process that brought events to this point and which will carry them further.

II

It is this dimension that was provided by Brian Manning's extensive work on the middling sort and the English revolution, originally pre-

---

[9] ibid., pp.3-4.
[10] ibid. pp.4-5.

sented in his pioneering *The English People and the English Revolution* in 1976. Manning's book appeared just as the revisionist current was gaining strength and it is fair to say that it received a mixed reception. Looking back in 1985, Buchanan Sharpe noted that, 'Since the appearance of Manning's work, even historians like [Anthony] Fletcher, committed to a largely elite perspective on the origins of the English Revolution, have been compelled to find a place for the people in the Revolution.' Sharpe was particularly impressed, as was Clive Holmes, by Manning's account of how the repeated mobilisation of the London crowd fuelled the polarisation that produced a more radical parliamentarianism and, in reaction, a Royalist party of order, thus paving the way to civil war. And he concluded that: 'There can be no doubt that Manning's book has made historians more aware of the people's place in the English Revolution even if it has not fundamentally altered mainstream views.' Manning himself, in his introduction to the second edition of *The English People and English Revolution,* noted similar more-or-less enthusiastic appreciation from David Underdown, Derek Hirst, Barry Reay, and Keith Wrightson.[11]

But criticism outweighed praise, and the tone was sometimes vituperative. This marred what were often well made points in, for instance, John Morrill's review. And an inordinate amount of Morrill's criticism seems to revolve around Manning's supposed over-reliance on printed rather than manuscript sources. Indeed, for Morrill, this was 'the essential reason for the failure of this book.' It's worth pausing for a moment to consider this for it's a frequently used argument against Christopher Hill as well. The element of truth in the argument, to which every historian can readily agree, is that it

[11] B. Manning, *The English People and the English Revolution*, pp.7-8. This analysis was extended and defended in B. Manning, 1649, *The Crisis of the English Revolution* (London, Bookmarks, 1992), B. Manning, *Aristocrats, Plebeians and Revolution in England, 1640-1660*, B. Manning, *The Far Left and the English Revolution*, B. Manning, *Revolution and counter-revolution in England, Ireland, and Scotland, 1658-1660* (London, Bookmarks, 2003). B. Sharpe, 'The Place of the People in the English Revolution', *Theory and Society*, Vol.14, No.1 (Jan. 1985) pp.96, 98. C. Holmes, review, *The American Historical Review*, Vol.82, No.1 (Feb. 1977), pp.96-7.

is best to use the widest range of sources available and that this will include printed material, manuscripts, but also, where appropriate, material objects, geographical data, weather reports and a host of other sources of information. But Morrill goes beyond this elementary point to insist that large amounts of printed material is simply propaganda which cannot be trusted: 'a convenient set of half-truths set forth by the polemicists on both sides.' This is simply not true. Not all printed material is propaganda, or not wholly or completely propaganda. Nor is all printed material by polemicists of the two extremes. Nearly all of it contains a mixture of fact and argument, often by those who are unaligned or reluctantly, or moderately, aligned. And even predominately propaganda material will contain vital factual information. Nor is it the case that we should necessarily see privately expressed views in manuscripts as more 'true' than publicly expressed views in printed material. Political actors may often utter half-formed prejudices in private which do not remotely accurately express their public positions, thus the public may be more 'true' than the private, more considered, closer to what any given actor may actually be realistically trying to achieve. Now, of course it would be a fine thing to always have both manuscript and printed sources to compare. But where that is impossible, as it so often is, there is no automatic reason for privileging the private over the public. Nor is there any reason for preordained distrust of recollections after the event. It is simply not the case that they are all 'the subsequent recollections of men all of whom looked back on 1640s with jaundiced eyes'. Indeed, the opposite may be true. People often see events more clearly when they recollect them later, understand more fully what was of significance and what not, than they do in the heat of the day.[12]

The substantial critical debate over Manning's approach revolved around a number of other issues. Clive Holmes thought that 'as a category of social analysis, the "middle sort of people" is so broad as to be amorphous'. And he also thought that Manning attributed a radical ideology to the middling sort as a whole and therefore ignored

[12] J. Morrill, 'Provincial Squires and "Middling Sorts" in the Great Rebellion', *The Historical Journal*, Vol.20, No.1 (Mar. 1977), pp.229-36, the quotation is from p.230.

the other political movements which encompassed the middling sort - peace petitioners in 1642-43, the Clubmen, London Presbyterian organisation. John Morrill made the same point, noting that the Clubmen were 'far more imposing' than the Levellers. Buchanan Sharpe agreed that Manning's middling sort was an 'elastic category … encompassing not only urban craftsmen and prosperous peasants but occasionally even urban wage earners and rural labourers.' Thus Manning left some 'lack of clarity in dealing with the relationship between the grievances of the labouring poor and those of the "middling sort".' Ian Gentles found fault because 'large numbers of lower class people - apprentices, butchers, porters, sailors and watermen in particular - were vehement in their hostility to the Independent Party and in their support for peace with the King.' These two issues, how the middling sort were to be defined and what the relationship was between the middling sort and politics, deserve further discussion.[13]

Defining the middling sort, as has already been noted, as with any intermediate class, does present some difficulties. But Manning himself responded to this problem with admirable clarity. The middling sort ranged, he wrote, 'from larger farmers (called "yeomen") and substantial tradesmen to the mass of land-holding peasants (called "husbandsmen") and self-employed craftsmen.' 'The range', Manning was clear, 'in wealth and social standing is very large between prosperous yeomen and tradesmen and the poor small-holding workers in agriculture and manufacture, and the whole social constellation only gains some coherence by demarcation from the gentry above them and the landless wage-labourers and paupers below them.' In part, the range was a product of how large a proportion of society the middling sort represented. Manning quotes Barry Reay's estimate that they comprised 30-40 percent of the population below the

[13] C. Holmes, *The American Historical Review*, review, Vol.82, No.1 (Feb. 1977), pp.96-7. B. Sharpe, 'The Place of the People in the English Revolution', pp.99, 104. J. Morrill, 'Provincial Squires and "Middling Sorts" in the Great Rebellion', p.231. For Manning's discussion of John Morrill, see B. Manning, *The English People and the English Revolution*, pp.27-9. I. Gentles, 'Soldiers, Levellers and the "Middle Sort" in the English Revolution', *Left History: An Interdisciplinary Journal of Historical Inquiry and Debate* 2, no.1 (1994).

level of the gentry, figures that correspond closely to Peter Earle's figures. So, whatever the difficulties of definition might be across such a large social group, their very weight in society makes it important that a working definition is arrived at and Manning, both in general and specifically, was able to do so. This, however, was a spur to engaging with the complexity of the issue, not a way of avoiding it. In an important passage in *Aristocrats, Plebeians and Revolution in England*, Manning wrote:

> 'The term "middle sort", however, is vague. It refers not only to bigger peasants and richer craftsmen but also to the general body of small producers in agriculture and industry who had sufficient resources to live without having to work for wages. It does not mean that a fully conscious capitalist class had already emerged and it is not synonymous with later usage of "middle class" and "bourgeoisie". The rising capitalists among the small producers were at least partially still enfolded within the broad mass of peasants, craftsman and traders. A bourgeoisie is in the process of formation and the appearance of the term "middling sort" prefigures this, but without divorcing them from the general body of small property-holders who still retain possession of the means of production - peasants, craftsman and traders. While it indicates a polarisation between the "middle sort" and, on the one hand, the aristocracy and, on the other hand, the poor, this was softened by association of the richer stratum with the minor gentry and by others experiencing poverty at various stages of their lives and at times of economic depression.'

This passage is important because it lays the basis for understanding some of the political alignments, between the middling sort and the lower gentry for instance, which are crucial for explaining the development of the revolution.[14]

Buchanan Sharpe was on stronger ground is his suggestion that

---

[14] B. Manning, *The English People and the English Revolution*, pp.7-8. B. Manning, *Aristocrats, Plebeians and Revolution in England*, 1640-1660, pp.10-11.

Manning sometimes incorporated sections of the rural poor into his middling-sort category when they were often from a different class background and were pursuing goals that were distinct from those middling-sort activists who were parliamentarian radicals. This is the case in the disafforestation struggles of the 1620s and 1640s, for instance, when parliamentarian leaders like John Pym and Edmund Ludlow were working for disafforestation against the interests of rural protestors, while others, like future radical MP Alexander Rigby, were acting for those contesting disafforestation. A better way of handling this phenomena would be to state more clearly the different class basis of the struggles of the rural poor and more carefully to delineate both the fact that they often took place against the same opponents that the middling sort faced, thus deepening the crisis faced by the authorities, and sometimes, but not always, drew some elements of the middling sort to their side, as the fenmen drew Lilburne and Wildman to represent them in the 1650s.[15]

This brings us to the second substantive criticism of Manning's approach: that he assumes too direct a link between the middling sort as a class and the political stances of parliamentary radicalism, ignoring the variety of ideologies to which the middling sort subscribed. Manning made a response to this in his introduction to the second edition of *The English People and the English Revolution*. He pointed out that he had always argued that there were 'numerous royalists among the trading and industrial classes', and that 'most of the people were neutral in the civil war'. These, however, were largely defensive formulations. Manning put a stronger positive case elsewhere:

> 'In no conflict in history do all, or even a majority, of one class line up on one side at all, or even a majority, or another class on the other; and in no conflict are there only members of one class on each side. Whether or not a conflict is a class conflict depends on the extent to which it involves class issues ...

[15] B. Sharpe, 'The Place of the People in the English Revolution', pp.105-9. Manning acknowledges this issue, see *The English People and the English Revolution*, pp.24-5.

> 'A whole class does not become radicalised or class conscious at once, and the "middle sort" in general lack the coherence to take a single class position. Groups become conscious of themselves as a class in the course of a conflict with other groups identifiable as different classes. Out of the diversity of the "middle sort" there emerged elements that, without being exactly the same as the growing capitalist or bourgeois tendency, became conscious of the difference between their economic and ideological position and that of others, and found themselves united to defend it against the party which they identified with the aristocracy or ruling class. Thus they reached the level of both radicalism and class consciousness.'[16]

So far then, we might say that Manning has acknowledged that more than one ideology existed among the middling sort – popular royalism, Presbyterianism, neutralism – as well as radical parliamentarianism. As importantly, he has outlined the dynamic and conflictual way in which the ideology of radical parliamentarianism took hold among sections of the middling sort as the revolution developed. But in another suggestive remark, he moves beyond these thoughts to explain why this ideological strand might be regarded as one of the most effective middling-sort political programmes. In acknowledging John Morrill's point that the middling sort were divided ideologically, Manning notes, 'that, of course, does not make them any less of a class, nor alter the fact that those of them who supported parliament were more effective in influencing events than those of them who supported the king'. The idea here is that, although it may be true that a variety of ideologies are present in any class, it is that ideology that most represents underlying class interests and most completely adapts to the political possibilities of the moment that will be the most effective. The middling sort among Royalists were always likely to play second fiddle to the aristocrats that were Royalism's most prominent supporters. Clubmen, no matter how valid their desire for peace, were battling a political reality more powerful than they were. Middling-sort radicals, on the

---

[16] B. Manning, *Aristocrats, Plebeians and Revolution in England*, p.71.

other hand, were at the very least cutting with the grain of one very powerful political dynamic and were also substantially representative of the interests of their fellows.[17]

III

There is however one important way in which we might improve on Manning's explanatory use of the 'middling sort'. I have already suggested that the risings of the rural poor might be better viewed as a distinct struggle which intersects with that of the middling sort in certain ways, rather than as a subset of the middling-sort struggles. In chapter 3, above, I have attempted to describe the way in which the Levellers tried to reach beyond their natural constituency, and in spite of important parts of their own ideology, to attract the support of the poor. In a like manner, and precisely because as Manning suggests, the middling sort shade into the lower gentry, it would be well to regard the relationship of the middling sort with the lower gentry, in particular their political representatives in parliament, in the same way.

The gentry and the middling sort were distinct economically, but they had some important overlapping interests. The economic basis of this was that some of the lower gentry were managing their estates along new, market-oriented lines. Even those that were not might well be affected by the new commercial environment that this development was creating and the political challenges it posed. One need not be a market-oriented landowner to react to political challenges in the way that those landowners who were reacted. It was on this basis that political co-operation, the construction of an effective political bloc, was possible: between the radicals who took over the City when Isaac Pennington became Mayor and radicals in the Commons for instance, later between Levellers and Independents. The need for such alliances made certain forms of cross-class ideology both necessary and effective: anti-Popery, radical Puritanism, resistance theory, Parliamentary sovereignty, to give just some examples. These were political projects to which a variety of

[17] B. Manning, 'Class and the English Revolution', *International Socialism*, No.38 (Spring 1988), p.47.

political actors might adhere irrespective their exact class origin. At the same time, they appealed most completely to a middling-sort constituency. They inspired and drove this group most effectively. Approached in this way, both the indispensable irreducibility of politics is maintained as well as the relationship between the political register and its social and economic context.

Chapter 5

The Levellers and the historians

Literary arguments about the Levellers and English Revolution are as old as the revolution itself. The Levellers and their opponents were famously prone to print. And before the dust had settled, Royalists, Cromwellian publicists, and Leveller sympathisers were all justifying the actions of their co-thinkers. Debate has hardly abated since. It might seem an obvious point, but the first barrier to the transmission of the history of the Levellers was the political reaction that culminated in the Restoration. The Levellers suffered persecution and political exclusion from the first days of the Republican regime. John Lilburne spent most of the 1650s in exile or in jail. Edward Sexby died in the Tower under Cromwell. William Walwyn had quietly slipped back into private life. Richard Overton disappeared from prominence.

The restoration of the monarchy in 1660 was even less conducive to the continued propagation of revolutionary ideas. Some regicides were executed. John Milton was lucky to escape the same fate. Henry Marten was imprisoned for the rest of his life. Only John Wildman continued to plot and prosper under the new King. And as the revolution suffered reverses, censorship returned. The radical literature from which we know so much about the Levellers was even more dangerous to print and distribute after 1660.

But was all this enough to snuff out the radical impulse of the revolution? Historians of very different persuasions have argued that it was. Blair Worden writes that: 'Over the first eight decades or so of the eighteenth century the Levellers almost vanished from public discussion.'[1] In the nineteenth century, the Levellers fared little

---

[1] B. Worden, 'The Levellers in history and memory, c.1660-1960' in M. Mendle (ed.), *The Putney Debates of 1647, the army the levellers and the English state* (Cambridge, CUP, 2001), p.267. The same argument is put in B. Worden, *Roundhead Reputations* (London, Penguin, 2001), Ch.12, 'The Levellers and the Left.'

better and, according to Worden, as 'a subject of historical scholarship the Levellers are a twentieth century discovery'.[2] In an article written early in his career, Christopher Hill made a similar point: 'For two centuries nothing was written on the events of 1640-60 that could improve on the comments of contemporary observers ... For a century and a half after the Restoration it was Clarendon's view of the great rebellion that prevailed.'[3]

Other historians have contested this view. A different approach to judging the ways in which the Leveller experience was sustained from the Restoration to the Exclusion Crisis is suggested by Tim Harris.[4] Harris reviews some of the ways in which Leveller ideas survived into the Restoration, but he also recalibrates the issue in an important way. He suggests that what was fundamentally novel about the Levellers was that they were 'a mass movement, perhaps the first of its kind in England to be organised on such a scale ....'[5] If we look at the period after the counter-revolution, Harris says, we can see the recurrence of some of these forms of action even where explicitly Leveller demands are not present.[6] This pushes the argument a little far since the mobilisations of the Exclusion crisis never had the revolutionary force of the Leveller mobilisations. But Harris is right to insist that the Levellers introduced into political life new methods of popular organisation and mobilisation as well as a new set of ideas. These methods were then available to others, whether they were as radical as or less radical than the Levellers. This 'tradition of organising' is as much part of the Leveller inheritance as the *Agreement of the People*.[7]

But Leveller ideas did persist as well. The words from Leveller Richard Rumbold's speech on the scaffold, 'no man ... comes into

---

2 B. Worden, 'The Levellers in history and memory, c.1660-1960', p.256.

3 C. Hill, 'The English Civil War Interpreted by Marx and Engels', pp.130-1.

4 T. Harris, 'The Leveller Legacy: from Restoration to the Exclusion Crisis' in M. Mendle (ed.), *The Putney Debates of 1647, the army the levellers and the English state.*

5 ibid. p.232.

6 ibid., pp.237-8.

7 Which is not to say that the Levellers themselves were not also drawing on earlier forms of oppositional politics.

the world with a saddle on his back, neither any booted and spurred to ride him,' were reprinted and then paraphrased by novelist Daniel Defoe. Editions of antiquarian Antony Wood's *Athenae Oxonienses, An Exact History of all the Writers and Bishops who have had their education at the most antient and famous University of Oxford* in the late seventeenth and early eighteenth centuries contained a lengthy account of Lilburne's life.[8] In 1710, Henry Hills jr., the son of the original Leveller printer Henry Hills, republished Lilburne's *The Triall of Lieut. Collonell John Lilburne* which his father had originally published in 1649.[9] In 1724, we have reports of 'enthusiastic Levellers who pulled down enclosures and sought equality.'[10] Ariel Hessayon has noted the 25-page entry on Lilburne in the *Biographia Britannica* and the hostile references to the Levellers by David Hume and Edmund Burke.[11]

Edward Vallance has uncovered a persistent influence of John Lilburne's politics on radicals in the 1700s. He concludes 'historians have undervalued the degree of intellectual sympathy and continuity between the radicalism of the seventeenth century and that of the eighteenth.'[12] For a later period, F K Donnelly writes that there has been a 'too ready

[8] A. Wood, *Athenae Oxonienses, An Exact History of all the Writers and Bishops who have had their education at the most antient and famous University of Oxford* (London, R. Knaplock, D. Midwinter and J. Tonson, MDCCXXI), Vol. II. The entry for Cuthbert Sydenham, who had himself written against Lilburne and in defence of Haselrigg and Cromwell, contains a lengthy account of Lilburne's life pp.171-4.

[9] *A view of part of the many Traiterous, Disloyal and Turn-about Actions of H. H. Senior* (1684), Wing (CD-Rom) V359. E. Vallance, 'Reborn John? The Eighteenth-century Afterlife of John Lilburne', in *History Workshop Journal*, No.74 (Autumn, 2012), p.15. Hills jr. was also advertising for sale other works by Lilburne.

[10] See G. P. Gooch, *The History of English Democratic Ideas in the Seventeenth Century* (Cambridge, 1898), p.359 n.5.

[11] A. Hessayon, 'Fabricating radical traditions', in M. Caricchio, G. Tarantino, eds., *Cromohs Virtual Seminars. Recent historiographical trends of the British Studies (17th-18th Centuries)*, 2006-2007: pp.1-6. http://www.cromohs.unifi.it/seminari/hessayon2_radical.html

[12] E. Vallance, 'Reborn John?', p.21.

acceptance of the discontinuity between the Levellers and the democrats of the post-1788 era.'[13] He points out that: 'Original Leveller pamphlets survived for a long time and were available in London in the 1790 to 1825 era.'[14] Jason McElligott has demonstrated the impact of Lilburne's work on London Corresponding Society activist William Hone and his fellow radical Jerimiah Joyce.[15] At about the same time, John Towill Rutt, the editor of the diary of Cromwellian MP Thomas Burton, included a note of five pages on Lilburne. He knew of Overton and wrote '*The Levellers* ... have probably been misrepresented and unjustly censured by contemporary historians,' and that they 'comprised a large body of Englishmen, of the finest sense, purest manners, and most enlightened religion.'[16] Donnelly and R C Richardson both point to the work of Catherine Macaulay, dismissed by Blair Worden as 'an isolated voice.'[17] Macaulay was a republican who personally owned some thirty Leveller tracts.[18] Donnelly thinks that eighteenth-century radicals knew about the Levellers but made less use of the heritage than they might have done precisely because of the hostility that the term invoked among their opponents, although there is also considerable evidence of a positive reception of the Levellers among supporters of John Wilkes.[19]

---

[13] F. K. Donnelly, 'Levellerism in Eighteenth and Early Nineteenth-Century Britain', *Albion* 20, 2 (Summer 1988), p.261.
[14] ibid. p.262.
[15] J. McElligott, 'William Hone (1780-1842), Print Culture and the Nature of Radicalism' in A. Hessayon and D. Finnegan (eds.), *Varieties of Seventeenth- and Early Eighteenth-Century Radicalism in Context* (Farnham, Ashgate, 2011), pp.241-61.
[16] T. Burton, *Diary of Thomas Burton, Esq. Member in the Parliaments of Richard and Oliver Cromwell, From 1656 to 1659*, edited by John Towill Rutt (London, Henry Colburn, 1828) in four volumes. See Vol. I, pp.49-50, Vol. III, pp.503-8.
[17] R. C. Richardson, *The Debate on the English Revolution* (London, Methuen,1977), pp.48-9. B Worden, 'The Levellers in history and memory, c.*1660*-1960', p.270.
[18] F. K. Donnelly, 'Levellerism in Eighteenth and Early Nineteenth-Century Britain', p.262. Macaulay published her eight volume *History of England from James I to the Brunswick Line* between 1763 and 1783.
[19] E. Vallance, 'Reborn John? ...', pp.16-17.

Certainly, the nineteenth century provided more fertile ground for Leveller ideas to be recalled. To some degree, this is because the experience of the French Revolution now played a larger part in radical ideology. It was through this accumulating experience of revolution that radicals, and their opponents, would look back at the English Revolution. This points to an important conclusion: historiography of the English Revolution should not be seen in a linear and national manner when it is in fact discontinuous and international.

I

The Levellers' message was less threatening to those who formed the first working-class and socialist currents in the nineteenth century. A 'very favorable exposition and defence of Levellerism', originally published in 1659, was reprinted in the Harleian Miscellany in 1810, made available to a wider audience in a collection of tracts published in 1840, and then carried in a Chartist newspaper.'[20] Indeed, some Chartists began to call for a rejection of the abusive use of 'Leveller': 'In 1842 two Chartist editors called for a revisionist, democratic approach to the understanding of the Levellers.' Chartist Henry Vincent's introduction to his reprint of the defence of the Levellers from 1659 began with this assessment: 'Hireling historians have conspired in representing the "Levellers" as a set of ignorant fanatics; but the following will evidence the atrocious villainy and utter falsehood of such an assumption.'[21] Marx and Engels, closely involved with the Chartist leaders, were not inhibited in their discussion of the English Revolution. In 1844 Engels was already comparing the French and English revolutions in these terms:

> 'The English revolution of the seventeenth century is nothing other than the prototype of the French revolution of 1789 ... Cromwell is Robespierre and Napoleon in one; the

---

[20] F. K. Donnelly, 'Levellerism in Eighteenth and Early Nineteenth-Century Britain', p.264.

[21] ibid., pp.268-9. The use of the term 'hireling' may be an echo of the Quaker use of the same term to describe priests.

> Presbyterians, Independents and Levellers appear as the Gironde, the Mountain and the Herbertists and Babouvists; in both cases the political results are rather lamentable and the whole parallel, which could have been drawn in still more precise terms, demonstrates at the same time that religious and irreligious revolutions, in as far as they remain political, finally amount to one and the *same thing*.'[22]

A few years later, Karl Marx was polemicising in his, 'A Review of Guizot's Book, *Why Has The English Revolution Been Successful?*' against a gradualist interpretation of the seventeenth century.[23] Blair Worden tends to talk as if socialists only became interested in the radical wing of the English revolution at the start of the twentieth century. But Marx, Engels and other Chartists were showing interest just as socialism emerged as a distinct current. With the retreat of these movements after 1848, the current was much diminished but re-emerged with the rise of the New Unions in Britain and the Second International in late 1880s. Marx and Engels are one important element of continuity throughout this period. In *Socialism Utopian and Scientific*, Engels argued, 'in every great bourgeois movement there were independent outbursts of that class which was the more or less developed forerunner of the modern proletariat. For example … in the great English Revolution, the Levellers.'[24] Earlier, Marx wrote: 'The first manifestation of a truly active communist party is contained within the bourgeois revolutions, at the moment when constitutional monarchy is eliminated. The most consistent *republicans* - in England the *Levellers*, in France the *Babeuf, Buonarotti,* etc - were the first to proclaim these "social questions".'[25] Marx

[22] F. Engels, 'The Position of England, The Eighteenth Century' in K. Marx and F. Engels, *Articles on Britain* (Moscow, Progress, 1975), pp.13-14.
[23] K. Marx, 'A Review of Guizot's Book, "Why Has The English Revolution Been Successful?"' in K. Marx and F. Engels, *Articles on Britain*, pp.88-95.
[24] F. Engels, *Socialism Utopian and Scientific* (London, Bookmarks, 1993), p.59. Engels interest in revolts against the feudal order was long-standing, see his *The Peasant War in Germany* (Moscow, Progress, 1977).
[25] K. Marx, 'Moralising Criticism and Critical Morality' in Karl Marx and

and Engels were careful not to overstate this issue, noting that the radical forces 'had no interests separate from the bourgeoisie' and that they did not 'form independent evolved classes or sub-classes.'[26]

In 1895, German socialist Eduard Bernstein, in exile in London and a close collaborator of Engels, published *Communist and Social-Democratic Currents in the English Revolution (Kommunistische und demokratisch-sozialistische Strömungen während der englischen Revolution)*. This book was part of a historical series initiated by Karl Kautsky under the title *Vorläufer des neueren Sozialismus (Forerunners of Modern Socialism)*. Bernstein accomplished this work some years before he developed the 'revisionist' interpretation of Marxism for which he is still best known.[27] The fourth edition was published in 1922 and it was this version that was eventually translated into English and published in 1930 with the far less accurate title of *Cromwell and Communism*.[28]

Blair Worden suggests that the Chartists were at least as much enamoured with Cromwell as they were with the Levellers. He quotes George Harney's *Red Republican* describing the 'spirit of Cromwellian might ... stirring at this hour.'[29] And he could have added Marx's report of a London mass meeting in 1855 where MP Apsley Pellant tried to flatter a working-class audience with a call to 'go about the tasks of reforming the government with determination, temperance, steadiness and the resolution of *Cromwell Ironsides*.'[30] There can be no doubt that a cult of Cromwell was under construction in the Vic-

Frederick Engels, *MECW*, Vol. 6, (London, Lawrence and Wishart, 1976), p.321. Also see C. Hill, 'The English Civil War Interpreted by Marx and Engels', p.144.

[26] See C. Hill, 'The English Civil War Interpreted by Marx and Engels', p.145.

[27] See D. W. Morgan, 'The Father of Revisionism Revisited', *Journal of Modern History*, 51 (1979), pp.525-32.

[28] E. Bernstein, *Cromwell and Communism* (Nottingham, Spokesman, 1980). See Ted Crawford's notes to the online edition at http://www.marx.org/reference/archive/bernstein/works/1895/cromwell/trans.htm

[29] B. Worden, 'The Levellers in history and memory, c.1660-1960', p.274.

[30] Quoted by K. Marx, 'A Meeting' in Karl Marx and Frederick Engels, *Articles on Britain*, p.228.

torian era. Thomas Carlyle brought out his *Oliver Cromwell's Letters and Speeches* in 1845. In it, he said Lilburne was the captain of 'a whole submarine world of Calvinistic Sansculottism, Five-point Charter and Rights of Man, threatening to emerge almost two centuries before its time!'[31] T. W. Mason records Chartist Henry Vincent lectured 'repeatedly over three decades on the exemplary moral virtues of Oliver Cromwell.'[32] Cromwell's statue at the Palace of Westminster was presented to Parliament by the then Prime Minister, Lord Rosebery, in 1895.[33]

There seems no need to counterpose renewed interest in Cromwell to continued interest in the Levellers. After all, Cromwell and the Levellers were, most of the time until 1649, allied on the radical wing of the revolution. *The Red Republican* might as well have been referring to the Cromwell who 'would as soon discharge my pistol' on the King 'as upon any private man' as it was likely to have been referring to Cromwell's suppression of the Levellers. Vincent, as we have seen, praised both. Liberals and the left looked to Cromwell, albeit for different reasons.[34]

---

[31] See A. Hessayon, 'Fabricating radical traditions.'

[32] T. W. Mason, 'Nineteenth-Century Cromwell', *Past and Present*, No.40 (July 1968), p.187.

[33] See www.parliament.uk/about/visiting/exhibitions/cromwell_conservation.cfm

[34] Leon Trotsky was still presenting a radical Cromwell in his 1925 remarks on the English Revolution in 'Where is Britain Going?' See L. Trotsky, *Trotsky's Writings on Britain*, Vol.2 (London, New Park, 1974), pp.85-93. Worden may be predisposed to see a greater tension here than there actually is, because he is reading back his own political preoccupations into the nineteenth century, perhaps even into the seventeenth century. He concludes his contribution to M. Mendle (ed.), *The Putney Debates of 1647* (Cambridge, CUP, 2001) with this remark: 'perhaps it is fitting that the 350th anniversary of the Putney debates was celebrated in two places: in Putney Church, with speeches by Christopher Hill and Tony Benn, representatives of the tradition that has looked east to Moscow; and, in the conference from which this book has emerged, in Washington, the capital of the free world.' Leaving aside the issue of what might be meant by 'the free world' and whether or not Washington is its capital, there is another problem with this formulation. There were some

II

What is true, is that for the whole of the eighteenth century and most of the nineteenth century, documents vital to understanding the Leveller legacy were either completely unknown or known mostly to scholars, booksellers and collectors. And, before the rise of the modern academic system, what was known generally about the English Revolution was transmitted through politically engaged writers who were liable to have an instrumental view of the knowledge they were popularising.

Two historians transformed this landscape: S R Gardiner (1829-1902) and C H Firth (1857-1936). Samuel Rawson Gardiner was a descendent of Oliver Cromwell through his eldest daughter Bridget and her husband Henry Ireton. He was from a liberal nonconformist background. Gardiner's monumental study of the English Revolution is, unlike any other work over 130 years old, still indispensable to modern historians.[35] Gardiner's approach was rigorously empirical and insistently chronological. Although Gardiner had a difficult relationship with academic institutions in his day - he did not have a paying University post until comparatively late in his career - his work set a new standard in scholarship. The notion of the Puritan Revolution at the heart of Gardiner's account remained the orthodoxy until the 1930s.[36]

---

on the left of the Labour Party who were sympathetic to Stalinism, but Tony Benn was not among them. And Christopher Hill famously and acrimoniously left the Communist Party precisely over its crushing of the 1956 Hungarian Revolution and the related question of its own internal democracy. In doing so, he contributed to the founding of the New Left which was highly critical of Stalinism. It seems odd that historians who would balk at failing to distinguish between a Particular Baptist and a General Baptist should be unable to bring the same care to the study of modern left politics. See B. Worden, 'The Levellers in history and memory, c.1660-1960', p.280.

[35] As Nicholas Tyacke says in his editor's introduction to *The English Revolution c.1590-1720, Politics, Religion and Communities* (Manchester, MUP, 2007), Gardiner's unrivalled command of sources produced an immensely detailed narrative that has 'broadly stood the test of time'. p.7.

[36] The most recent publication of eight of the eighteen volumes of Gar

Charles Firth discovered and prepared for publication the manuscripts left behind by the secretary to the General Council of the New Model Army, William Clarke. This extraordinary record of the New Model Army debates, including the then unknown Putney Debates, transformed the historical record of the revolution at its decisive point. Firth, a friend and colleague of Gardiner, let him see the material as it was being prepared for publication and Gardiner incorporated it into his *History*. As Gardiner recorded in his Preface 'Mr Firth's discovery of the *Clarke Papers* throws every other accession of material into the shade.'[37] The Camden Society published the first volume of the *Clarke Papers* in 1891. They still have the capacity to astound modern historians. When the Camden Society's first two volumes of the *Papers* were reissued over 100 years later, Austin Woolrych's preface noted: 'one may wonder whether there has ever in modern times been a more exciting archival discovery in any field of British history. Its fascination has spread far beyond the ranks of professional historians; surely no other seventeenth century source is more widely read ….'[38]

Gardiner and Firth's work suddenly provided a version of the English Revolution's broad historical meaning dramatised with the voices of the revolutionaries themselves. The central role of army radicals and the Levellers, the full scale of the transformation of English society that they debated, was now known in a way in which it had not been before. Eduard Bernstein, who had a very different outlook, quoted Gardiner and Firth as authorities and spoke of Gardiner's 'outstanding work.'[39] Quaker and radical Lewis H. Berens

diner's history was made by the Windrush Press between 1987 and 1989. The first four volumes are S. R. Gardiner, *History of the Great Civil War* and remaining four are S. R. Gardiner, *History of the Commonwealth and Protectorate.*

[37] S. R. Gardiner, *History of the Great Civil War*, Vol. I (London, Windrush, 1987), p.ix.

[38] A. Woolrych, 'Preface to the 1992 Edition' in W Clarke, *The Clarke Papers* (edited and introduced by C. H. Firth, London, Royal Historical Society, 1992). There is no pagination for the Woolrych's Preface but these remarks are on the first page.

[39] E. Bernstein, *Cromwell and Communism*, p.11. The remarks are made

made good use of the *Clarke Papers* in his 1906 study.[40] Theodore Pease was, after Bernstein, the next to produce a book-length study devoted to the Levellers. His *The Leveller Movement* was based on research of the Thomason Tracts in the British Museum in 1911, although the book was not published until 1916. He benefitted from the fact that the *Catalogue of the Thomason Tracts* had been printed in 1908. Pease said that Gardiner's volumes 'of course have the claim to prior mention'.[41]

This first wave of modern scholars on the radicals of the English Revolution came from politically heterogeneous backgrounds. Bernstein stood, at this point, in the dead centre of the Marxist orthodoxy of the Second International. His work is valuable because it is the first book-length study of the Levellers and Diggers that situates their struggle in the wider social and economic conflicts of their day. It also understands them as active revolutionaries, people whose foremost affiliation was to an organised group of militants attempting a rudimentary collective political challenge to the existing order.

Lewis Berens' analysis bears the marks of two traditions. The first, and the one that has the greatest impact on the substantive core of his book, is his religious affiliation as a Quaker. The second and lesser influence, although it is declared loudly in the conclusion of the book, is his admiration for American radical Henry George (1839-97). George, influential in his day, regarded the land as the common inheritance of humanity. A socialist in only the broadest sense, George was described by Marx as a 'writer with talent' but whose economic theories were 'utterly backward'.[42] In the fundamentals of their approaches, Berens and Bernstein had little in

in an introduction to editions later than the original 1895 publication. There is, however, no specific date on for the introduction itself.

[40] L. H. Berens, *The Digger Movement in the Days of the Commonwealth* (Monmouth, Merlin, 2007).

[41] T. C. Pease, *The Leveller Movement* (Gloucester, Mass., Peter Smith, 1965), p.367.

[42] K. Marx, 'Marx to Friedrich Adolph Sorge in Hoboken' in *K. Marx and F. Engels, Selected Correspondence* (Moscow, Progress, 1955), pp.322-3. See also the discussion of Berens and George in J. Gurney, *Gerrard Winstanley* (London, Pluto, 2013), p.116.

common, although both did see long-term causes of the English Revolution running back to the Reformation.

The History of English Democratic Ideas in the Seventeenth Century, published in 1898, came from the pen of George Peabody Gooch. Later, in 1906, Gooch was elected Liberal MP for Bath and, in the 1930s, president of the National Peace Council. His book was read before publication by Gardiner and made full use of the *Clarke Papers*. Although it is devoted to the idea of democratic progress culminating in Victorian parliamentarianism, it also concludes by arguing that as the founder of modern socialism, Robert Owen, was 'directly descended from the thinkers of the Interregnum'.[43] And as Felix Hirsch remarks, 'His treatment of the Communists of those days, especially Winstanley, was so novel that this chapter was translated into Russian, after the Bolsheviks came to power. That meant, on their part, quite a compliment to such a liberal bourgeois as Gooch.'[44]

Theodore Pease was an American academic. His *The Leveller Movement* concentrates more centrally on the Leveller movement than Bernstein or Gooch. Pease is careful to cite the political context of the movement, but there is a strong accent on the Levellers as the creators of a written constitution. Pease stands at the heart of the American liberal tradition, more Whig than the British original:

> '...the Levellers developed a body of constitutional and political doctrines that suggest the main theories of American constitutional law. The sovereignty of the people, the inalienable right of the individual, the binding force of paramount law, the enforcement of political law by judicial action - all of these are American doctrines.'[45]

Thus in this first wave of modern scholarship, three of the four main currents of later analysis are represented: the left's social and

---

[43] G. P. Gooch, *The History of English Democratic Ideas in the Seventeenth Century*, p.vi and p.360.

[44] F. E. Hirsch, 'George Peabody Gooch', *The Journal of Modern History*, Vol.26, No.3 (Sep. 1954), p.263. See also F. Eyck, 'Gooch, George Peabody (1873-1968)', *ODNB*.

[45] T. C. Pease, *The Leveller Movement*, p.363.

economic framework, the religious dimension and liberal political theory. What is not yet present is a modern academic current which attempts to diminish the Levellers' influence on the revolution. At this time, none of the writers specifically about the Levellers and Diggers are English: Bernstein is German, Berens and Pease are American. Even the journalist and admirer of Winstanley, John Morrison Davidson, was Scottish.[46] This suggests that where some look for the continuity of Leveller and radical influence only in England, we would be wise to widen the search.

In its origins and early years, the English Revolution was connected to America, just as American scholars were later vital to recording its history. America and the West Indies were important to the radicals before the revolution as sanctuary from Stuart persecution. John Winthrop, the first Governor of Massachusetts, was married to Martha Rainsborough, sister of Leveller Thomas Rainsborough. It was from the other side of the Atlantic that many returned to fight in the New Model Army. Winthrop's son, Stephen, was a captain in the regiment of William Rainsborough, Leveller and brother of Thomas. William himself came back from America to fight in the civil war.[47] Stephen Winthrop, like his father, married a Rainsborough sister. It was to America and the West Indies that many went in the 1650s and after the Restoration. Both William Rainsboroughs, Thomas's brother and son, went to Boston after the revolution. Henry Marten's brother George was in Barbados in 1647 and in *Oroonoko*, Aphra Behn, despite her royalism, praised him as 'a man of great gallantry, wit and goodness … wise and eloquent'.[48] Regicides William Goffe, Edward Whalley,

---

[46] H. C. G. Matthew, 'John Davidson', *ODNB*. J Gurney, *Gerrard Winstanley* (London, Pluto, 2013), p.5, 116.

[47] C. G. Pestana, 'Rainborowe, William (fl. 1639-1673), *ODNB* (Oxford, 2004).

[48] See C. Hill, 'Radical Pirates', in *Collected Essays*, vol.3 (Brighton, Harvester 1986), pp.165-75. H. R. Williamson, *Four Stuart Portraits* (London, Evans Brothers, 1949), p.110. Aphra Behn, *Oroonoko and other stories* (Koln, Konemann, 1999), p.73. George Marten was in Suriname after his time in Barbados. Behn visited the English sugar colony in Suriname while in her twenties. Behn's play, The Younger Brother has George Marten as a central character.

and John Dixwell fled to New England where they were welcomed as heroes and protected from capture by the colonists.[49]

The Puritan and radical current fed into the American Revolution. As one account of the revolution records, 'Country folk … said little before 1774. But farm families christened newborn boys Oliver, after Cromwell, showing what they were thinking.'[50] One such personal connection can be traced through the family of Thomas Jefferson himself:

> 'Jefferson's maternal grandfather was Isham Randolph and in 1717 at Shadwell Parish Church in London he married Jane Lilburne, a first-cousin descendant of Freeborn John. Isham and Jane had two daughters: one married Peter Jefferson (father of Thomas) who named his Virginia family home Shadwell … The second daughter of Isham and Jane married Charles Lewis who named a son Charles Lilburne Lewis. That son married Lucy Jefferson, sister of Thomas and they named a son Lilburne Lewis. Randolph Jefferson (brother of Thomas and Lucy) named a son Lilburne Jefferson. In 1790 Thomas Jefferson's daughter Martha (Patsy) married her second cousin Thomas Mann Randolph and they established their Virginia home at Edgehill. The house was named after the site of the first major battle in the English Civil Wars ….'[51]

In 1826, Jefferson quoted the Leveller epigram from Richard Rumbold's scaffold speech.[52]

---

[49] See C. Durston, 'Goffe, William (d.1679?)', *ODNB* (Oxford, 2004) and C. Durston, 'Whalley, Edward, appointed Lord Whalley under the protectorate (d. 1674/5)', *ODNB*. Also E. Stiles, *A History of Three Judges of Charles I* (Hartford, Conn., 1794). Others, like Edmund Ludlow, fled to Europe. See C. H. Firth, 'Ludlow, Edmund (1616/17–1692)', and B. Worden, *ODNB* entry.

[50] B. Levine, S. Brier, D. Brundage, E. Countryman, D. Fennell, M. Rediker, *Who Built America? Working People and the Nation's Economy, Politics, Culture and Society*, Vol. I (New York, Pantheon, 1989), p.149.

[51] See http://www.johnlilburne.com/reference/johnlilburne.html

[52] See C. Hill, *The Experience of Defeat, Milton and Some Contemporaries*

III

The single greatest wave of publication of Leveller writings, since the Levellers themselves burst into print in the 1640s, took place from the late 1930s through to the end of the 1940s. It is not difficult to trace the social conditions which influenced this revival. The impulse of the Russian Revolution led to the establishment of mass Communist Parties in Europe. Even the relatively small British CP was many times bigger, and more effective, than any of the socialist groupings that existed before the First World War.[53] But the inter-war era was also the time when the Labour Party really became established as the dominant organisation in the British working class.

The slump and the threat of fascism in the 1930s strengthened the counter-current of radicalism in British society, even if it failed to influence the course adopted by the governing elite. The fragility of European parliamentary democracy in the face of fascism, the collapse of appeasement in Britain, the experience of war, all led to the re-ignition of a profound egalitarian impulse among wide swathes of British people and to a questioning of what democracy would deliver in the post-war world.[54] In the US, the slump of the 1930s was more severe than in Britain, and the period of the New Deal had popularised egalitarian notions in a way that had not been the case since the Civil War and would not be true again until the civil-rights movement of the 1960s.[55]

From and into this environment, a mass of publications about

(London, Faber, 1984), p.37.

[53] See R. Challinor, *The Origins of British Bolshevism* (London, Croom Helm, 1977).

[54] On the background to this period see for instance E. Hobsbawm, *The Age of Extremes* (London, Michael Joseph, 1994), Chs.1-7. J. Stevenson and C. Cook, *The Slump, Society and Politics during the Depression* (London, Quartet, 1977). N. Branson and M. Heinemann, *Britain in the Nineteen Thirties* (St. Albans, Panther, 1973).

[55] See, for instance, H. Brogan, *Longman History of the United States of America* (London, Longman, 1985), H. Zinn, *A People's History of the United States* (London, Longman, 1980), esp. Chs.15 and 16, and E. Hobsbawm, *Age of Extremes*, esp., Ch.5.

the Levellers flowed. In 1938, A. S. P. Wodehouse published a selection of texts from the *Clarke Papers*, including the Putney Debates, under the title *Puritanism and Liberty* (1938). Published in the same year, A. L. Morton's *A People's History of England* contained a chapter on the Levellers. On the eve of war, Henry Holorenshaw produced *The Levellers and the English Revolution* (1939) as part of The New People's Library series published, like Morton's *People's History*, by CP publisher Victor Gollancz.[56] Gollancz was busy again in 1940 publishing David Petegorsky's study of the Diggers, *Left Wing Democracy in the English Civil War*, as a Left Book Club edition. Originally a doctoral dissertation at the University of London, the subject of the book was first suggested to Petegorsky by Harold Laski, co-founder of the Left Book Club and, after the war, Chairman of the Labour Party.[57] One only has to recall the situation in which Petegorsky wrote his preface in May 1940 - France lost, the Dunkirk evacuation, the Home Guard training to repel a German invasion - to understand the full meaning of the title of Petegorsky's book.[58] George Orwell's introduction to his 1948 co-edited collec-

[56] Henry Holorenshaw was a pen name of Joseph Needham, scientist, China expert and Marxist. Joseph Needham helpfully supplied a forward for 'my friend' Henry Holorenshaw's book on the Levellers.

[57] D. Petegorsky, *Left Wing Democracy in the English Civil War* (London, Gollancz, 1940), Preface. Laski had already edited the 1927 reprint of Gooch's *The History of English Democratic Ideas in the Seventeenth Century*.

[58] Tom Wintringham, founder of the *Daily Worker* and *Left Review*, veteran of the Spanish Civil War, left the CP in 1938 when his wife was accused of being a Trotskyist spy. He formed the first Home Guard units and trained them in tactics learnt in Spain, although the government would never let him into the official Home Guard when it was formed because of his left-wing politics. His book *Mutiny. Mutinies from Spartacus to Invergordon* (London, Stanley Nott, 1936) contained a chapter on the Levellers. In 1948, George Orwell, also a veteran of Spain, edited with Reginal Reynolds the volume *British Pamphleteers, Vol.1, From the Sixteenth Century to the French Revolution*. In his introduction Orwell wrote: 'The English Diggers and Levellers . . . are links in a chain of thought which stretches from the slave revolts of antiquity, through various peasant risings and heretical sects of the Middle Ages, down to the Socialists of the nineteenth

tion of *British Pamphleteers*, which included Leveller tracts, is very much of this moment.[59]

Two crucial selections of Leveller pamphlets came out of the US at the same time in 1944. It is testimony to the amount of unpublished Leveller material that lay in the archives that Don Wolfe's *Leveller Manifestos of the Puritan Revolution* and William Haller and Godfrey Davies' *The Leveller Tracts* 1647-1653 reproduced a total of 35 pamphlets only four of which were duplicates. M. A. Gibb did the work for the first book-length biography of Lilburne, *John Lilburne The Leveller*, before the war, but it only appeared in 1947. And in the same year *John Wildman, Plotter and Postmaster*, Maurice Ashley's reconstruction of the life of the Leveller leader was also published.[60] The following year, the torrent was joined by Wilhelm Schenk's *The Concern for Social Justice in the Puritan Revolution*.[61] In 1949, Hugh Ross Williamson provided the first twentieth-century study of the life of Thomas Rainsborough as one of his *Four Stuart Portraits*.[62]

Christopher Hill's much reproduced pamphlet 'The English Revolution 1640' originally appeared for the anniversary of the revolution in 1940 in a short book with the subtitle 'Three Essays of Interpretation'. The other two contributions were Margaret James' 'Contemporary Materialist Interpretations of Society in the English Revolution', which cited the Levellers and Winstanley, and Edgell

century and the Trotskyists and Anarchists of our own day.' This was, of course, a calculated insult to the Communist Party. See P. Bounds, 'Orwell and Englishness: The Dialogue with British Marxism', *Cultural Logic, An Electronic Journal of Marxist Theory and Practice* (2007), at http://clogic.eserver.org

[59] G. Orwell and R. Reynolds (eds.), *British Pamphleteers, Vol. I, From the sixteenth century to the Fench Revolution* (London, Allan Wingate, 1948).

[60] M. Ashley, John Wildman, *Plotter and Postmaster, A study of the English Republican Movement in the Seventeenth Century* (London, Jonathan Cape, 1947).

[61] W. Schenk, *The Concern for Social Justice in the Puritan Revolution* (London, Longmans, 1948).

[62] Only predated by E. Peacock, 'Notes on the Life of Thomas Rainsbourgh', *Archaeologia* 46 (1880).

Rickword's 'Milton: The Revolutionary Intellectual'.[63] In 1949, Christopher Hill and future Labour government minister Edmund Dell edited a collection of source material, *The Good Old Cause*, which contained a separate chapter of Leveller material.[64] The Communist Party Historians' Group was formed in 1946. It grew out of a conference called to discuss Morton's *A People's History*. In 1952, this group were a largely responsible for the launch of the journal *Past and Present*.[65]

Slightly outside this period, but very much a product of the scholarship and publications that it produced, is Joseph Frank's, *The Levellers, A History of the Writings of Three Seventeenth Century Social Democrats John Lilburne, Richard Overton, William Walwyn* (1955). Nearly everything about this title, apart from the words 'the Levellers', is misleading. Frank does not argue that Lilburne, Overton and Walwyn are 'social democrats' in either the nineteenth-century meaning (i.e. Marxist revolutionaries) or in the twentieth-century meaning (i.e. Labour Party type reformists) of this phrase. Neither is Frank's history a serial account of the writings of Lilburne, Overton and Walwyn. This could be more accurately said of Pease's book, which does trace the evolution of Leveller political thought through their writings. Precisely the strength of Frank's book is that it is the first major study to deal with the Levellers as an organised political movement. Leveller writings are placed in the context of a dynamic political situation in which the variations between texts were as likely

---

[63] C. Hill, M. James, E. Rickword, *Three Essays in Interpretation, The English Revolution 1640* (London, Lawrence and Wishart, 1940).

[64] C. Hill and E. Dell (eds.), T*he Good Old Cause, The English Revolution of 1640-1660, Its Causes, Courses and Consequences* (London, Frank Cass, 1949).

[65] For accounts of the CP Historians' Group see H. Kaye, *The British Marxist Historians* (Cambridge, Polity, 1995), S. Ashman, 'The Communist Party Historians' Group' in J Rees (ed.), *Essays on Historical Materialism* (London, Bookmarks, 1998) and D. Parker (ed.), *Ideology, Absolutism and the English Revolution, debates of the British Communist Historians* (London, Lawrence and Wishart, 2008). R. Samuel, 'British Marxist Historians, 1880–1980: Part One', *New Left Review* 120 (1980), and E. Hobsbawm, 'The Historians' Group of the Communist Party', pp.21-47.

to be a result of the pressures from opposed political currents and temporary allies as they were to be evolved constitutional thoughts. It is in this way that Frank profited from and incorporated the social and political work that had been done on the Leveller movement in the preceding decades. Neither are these strengths vitiated by Frank's evident concern with the McCarthy Trials taking place in the US at the time he wrote and to which he alludes. Frank does not make this the organising principle of his book. Indeed he refers to this context sparingly.

What were the main characteristics of this enormous outpouring of material about the Levellers? Firstly, the main traditions identified from the late nineteenth century are all still present - Christian (often non-conformist), liberal and left, including Marxist. Margaret Gibb's biography of Lilburne carried the subtitle 'A Christian Democrat' and of all the work published in this period, it has the greatest concern with the religious dimension of Leveller thought. Godfrey Davies, co-editor of *The Leveller Tracts 1647-1653*, had worked with C. H. Firth and can legitimately be seen as working within Gardiner's 'great tradition'. T. C. Pease's review of Haller and Davies certainly welcomed this edition, and D. M. Wolfe's compilation, as an extension of his own 1916 liberal interpretation of the Levellers.[66] Joseph Frank's book, the most impressive account of the Levellers to have emerged up to this point, stood in the mainstream of the liberal-democratic tradition. Morton, Holorenshaw (the pen name of Joseph Needham), Hill, Petegorsky, and Dell were all from the Communist Party, the left of the Labour Party, or held views compatible with these political positions.[67] Many of these writers shared a nonconformist background, like Berens, Hill, Brailsford and E. P. Thompson. Others, like Tawney, were Christian Socialists. Petegorsky, like Marx himself, came from a Jewish background.

Secondly, whatever the ideological inclinations of the authors,

---

[66] T. C. Pease, *The American Historical Review*, Vol.50, No.2 (Jan. 1945), pp.315-16.

[67] Hill's views were certainly influenced by his study in Moscow of Soviet historians' treatments of the English Revolution, although he was far from uncritical of them. See C. Hill, 'Soviet Interpretations of the English Interregnum', *Economic History Review*, No.8 (1938), pp.159-67.

they all drew from their environment a deep concern with the fate of democracy. Margaret Gibb's introduction to *John Lilburne*, her attention to the religious dimension of Lilburne's thought notwithstanding, is permeated with the concern that 'modern liberal democracy ... today stands under judgement' because it has produced a 'Monopoly Capitalism' that results in the 'exploitation of human need for the self-aggrandisement of the great combines'. It was this which meant that 'today ... it is particularly apposite to look back at that moment when it first emerged as a potential system of government, in the Leveller Movement.'[68] Whatever the exact political viewpoint of the main authors, the general spectrum of opinion had moved left in the 1930s and 1940s.

Thirdly, the weight of the left, particularly the Marxist left, was greater than it had been in the past. But it still did not predominate. And the presence of Marxist and left analyses was more marked in relation to the Levellers and the radicals of the English Revolution than it was in relation to the analysis of the Revolution as a whole. Variants of the Whig or liberal interpretation of the English Revolution were still dominant. Christopher Hill recalls: 'When I started out as a historian the orthodoxy was that England was the centre of world history and that the whole of history was working towards the evolution of democracy of which England was the perfect example. That's the thing my generation were gunning for - Anglo-centrism and concentration almost exclusively on political and constitutional history.'[69]

There were, of course, debates and arguments both between and within these broad currents of opinion. Winthrop Hudson, reviewing the Haller and Davies and the Wolfe collections in *Church History*, posted two objections to the editors' views of the Levellers. Firstly, the 'editors of both volumes make much of the fact that the Leveller movement was secular and not religious in character. They speak of the "secular philosophy" of the leaders and of the "secular Reformation" the Levellers were seeking to achieve. It is rather diffi-

---

[68] M. A. Gibb, *John Lilburne The Leveller, A Christian Democrat* (London, Lindsay Drummond, 1947), pp.12-14.

[69] Christopher Hill in L. Humber and J. Rees, 'The Good Old Cause - an interview with Christopher Hill', *International Socialism* 56 (London, 1992), p.126.

cult to discover the basis for this characterisation, for Lilburne's agitators were religious men, "animated by religious convictions"'. And a 'second minor misinterpretation to be found in both introductions is the conception that Winstanley and the Diggers embarked on a program of economic reform and summoned men to reconstruct society after a communist pattern. Winstanley was an apocalypticist.'[70] And while Hudson was critical of those he felt underplayed the religious dimension of Leveller and Digger thought, Christopher Hill pointed out that Henry Holorenshaw was 'exaggerating "socialist" tendencies among the Levellers'.[71]

C. L. R. James' enthusiastic welcome for the publication of Leveller manifestoes went onto make an important and little remarked upon point about the Marxist attitude to the radicals of the English Revolution. James argued that interest in the Levellers had been pioneered by liberal historians whereas those historians associated with the official Communist Parties had been more interested in the Diggers. The record of publication bears this out. Of the three major histories of the Levellers, two, Pease and Frank, were written by liberals and the third author, Brailsford, discussed below, was an anti-Stalinist Labour left. Hill had left the CP by the time he edited Brailsford's book for publication in 1961. James traced this fact back to the bureaucratisation of the communist movement under Stalin and its lack of sympathy for active revolutionary movements in comparison with 'communist' utopias.[72]

---

[70] W. S. Hudson, *Church History*, Vol. 14, No. 2 (Jun. 1945), pp.132-3. See also W. Hudson, 'Economic and Social Thought of Gerrard Winstanley: Was he a Seventeenth Century Marxist?' in *The Journal of Modern History*, Vol.18, No.1 (March 1946), pp.1-21.

[71] See 'Books for further reading' in C. Hill, M. James, E Rickword, *Three Essays in Interpretation, The English Revolution 1640*, p.135. The same point can be made about the title of Fenner Brockway's *Britain's First Socialists* (London, Quartet, 1980).

[72] C. L. R. James (writing as G.F. Eckstein), 'Ancestors of the Proletariat' in *Fourth International*, Vol. 10 No. 8, September 1949, pp.252-5 (available at http://www.marxists.org/archive/james-clr/works/1949/09/english-revolution.htm). Also see 'Cromwell and the Levellers', *Fourth International*, Vol.10, No.5 (May 1949), pp.143-8 (http://www.marxists.org/archive/james-clr/works/1949/05/english-revolution.htm).

This was an era of enormous creativity and it laid the basis for much scholarship down to the present day - whether subsequent historians agreed or not with the account being developed by Marxists, the left, and liberal historians. Leaving aside the broader work on the nature of the English Revolution, what we know specifically about the Levellers and other radicals is from work that built directly on the foundations laid in this period.

In 1961, two crucial works on the Levellers were published – H. N. Brailsford's *The Levellers and the English Revolution* and Pauline Gregg's biography of Lilburne, *Free-Born John*.[73] Brailsford died in 1958 leaving the almost completed manuscript of the *The Levellers* to be prepared for publication by Christopher Hill. Brailsford had led a remarkable life. The son of a Methodist preacher, he was already a well-known foreign correspondent for the *Manchester Guardian* in the 1890s. Brailsford was a stalwart of the Independent Labour Party and stood, unsuccessfully, as a Labour candidate in 1918. He visited Russia twice in 1920 and was sympathetic to the Russian Revolution, but in the 1930s he was one of the few writers associated with the Left Book Club who was consistently critical of the Stalin show trials. In *The Levellers*, Brailsford concentrated the accumulated wealth of knowledge that had formed in the liberal and left currents since Gardiner. Towards Gardiner and Firth, Brailsford said, he felt a 'gratitude that borders on veneration'. He had, he said, 'the good fortune to count' Eduard Bernstein 'as my friend' and he regarded Bernstein as 'the forerunner of us all'.[74] To his 'old friend' R. H. Tawney, and to G. P. Gooch and Margaret James, Brailsford gave thanks for helping him to 'organise my picture of the social background of Cromwell and the Levellers'. But the 'chief of my debts', wrote Brailsford, were to the 'pioneering work in recent years' by Pease, Haller and Davies, Wolfe, Petegorsky, Wodehouse and M. A. Gibb.[75]

Brailsford's was the first book-length account to fully integrate

---

[73] H. N. Brailsford (Christopher Hill ed.), *The Levellers and the English Revolution* (Nottingham, Spokesman, originally the Cresset Press, 1961). P. Gregg, *Free-Born John* (London, Dent, 1961).

[74] H. N. Brailsford, *The Levellers and the English Revolution*, p.xiii.

[75] ibid. pp.xii-xiii.

the economic, social and religious background of the Levellers with a description of the political dynamic of the revolution, the Levellers' role as an organised revolutionary current within it, and an estimate of the ideological advances that Leveller thought represented. If nothing else, it was a considerable work of synthesis. But it was more than this. Throughout the book, but particularly in the chapters on 'The Leveller Party' and 'The Moderate', Brailsford presented more forcefully than any writer before him a picture of the Levellers as a functioning political organisation of a quite new type.

Brailsford also had an eye for the telling detail. Just one example will suffice. There is an ongoing debate about whether or not the Leveller name was accepted or rejected by the movement. We know it began life as an insult directed at Lilburne and his comrades by their opponents. And we know that in official pronouncements, the Levellers distanced themselves from the name, and certainly from the accusation that they meant to level citizens economically. But Brailsford's study of the *Moderate* caught its account of the inscription on Rainsborough's grave:

> Rainsborough the just, the valiant and the true,
> Here bids the noble Levellers adieu.[76]

So, by 1648, the *Moderate* and supporters of the Levellers at Rainsborough's funeral, a major occasion for the party, were using the name positively.[77]

Pauline Gregg's life of Lilburne was cast in the same foundry as Brailsford's book. It benefitted from the same accumulation of scholarship and it shared Brailsford's concern to illuminate the social and economic background of the Leveller movement. And again, like Brailsford, Gregg described the Levellers as a political organisation.

---

[76] H. N. Brailsford, *The Levellers and the English Revolution*, p.310. A valuable related use of the Moderate to gauge the views of the Leveller movement is contained in R. Howell, Jr. and D. E. Brewster, 'Reconsidering the Levellers: The Evidence of the Moderate', *Past and Present*, no.46 (Feb. 1970), pp.68-86.

[77] Contrary to Andrew Sharpe's assertion in his introduction to A. Sharpe (ed.), *The English Levellers* (Cambridge, CUP, 1998), p.xxii.

One way of seeing the distance travelled since M. A. Gibb's biography is to compare her chapter on Lilburne as 'Leader of the Levellers' with Gregg's chapter 'Party Leader'.[78] Only in Gregg's account does the issue of political organisation appear as a subject of serious discussion. Gibb is more concerned with the political content of Lilburne's pamphlets at the height of the Leveller movement.

This social interpretation of the English Revolution developed throughout the 1960s and 1970s in the work of Christopher Hill, Brian Manning, A. L. Morton, Norah Carlin and others.[79] It is hard to reconcile this record of publication in the 1960s and 1970s with the account in one of the most sustained critiques of Marxist histories of the English Revolution, Alastair MacLachlan's *The Rise and Fall of Revolutionary England*. To speak only of Hill, any period that includes the publication of his *The Century of Revolution 1603-1714*, *Reformation to Industrial Revolution* and *God's Englishman* cannot be accurately described as merely 'Saving Appearances' in the Marxist account of the revolution.[80]

There were, of course, serious debates between Marxists and non-Marxists and among Marxists during this period. The left analysis was never unchallenged. Howard Shaw's popular 1968 textbook, *The Levellers*, for instance, concluded with a compendium of arguments that were later the mainstays of revisionism. Shaw wrote:

---

78 M. A. Gibb, *John Lilburne*, pp.160-87. P Gregg, *Freeborn John*, pp.226-37.

79 Christopher Hill's publications during this period include *The Century of Revolution 1603-1714* (Wokingham, Van Nostrand, Reinhold, 1961), *Reformation of Industrial Revolution* (London, Pelican, 1967), *God's Englishman* (London, Pelican, 1970), *The World Turned Upside Down* (London, Penguin, 1972). A. L. Morton's work included, *The World of the Ranters* (London, Lawrence and Wishart, 1970) and *Freedom in Arms, A Selection of Leveller Writings* (London, Lawrence and Wishart, 1974). Brian Manning, *The English People and the English Revolution*. Norah Carlin, 'Marxism and the English Civil War', *International Socialism*, No.10 (1980).

80 A. MacLachlan, *The Rise and Fall of Revolutionary England* (Basingstoke, Macmillan, 1996), Ch.4.

> 'In the last analysis, the Levellers' failure was due to their inability to stir the lower classes on their own behalf ... the vast bulk of the population was socially conservative and politically apathetic ... The Civil War itself ... had been an internecine struggle among the propertied classes. The ordinary people had on the whole been disinterested spectators ... The Levellers did their best to counteract this political illiteracy ... In London and the army ... they achieved temporary success; elsewhere the Leveller dream was shared by too few and feared by too many.

He concluded with this assessment: 'What, if anything, did the Levellers contribute to posterity? In a sense, very little ... "they had", in the words of Dr Schenk, "much more in common with William Langdale than with Thomas Paine or Karl Marx"'.[81]

Naturally, some elements of the left analysis of the 1940s had been significantly altered by the 1970s. One such debate that concerned the Levellers was begun in 1962 by C. B. Macpherson in *The Political Theory of Possessive Individualism.*[82] MacPherson argued that the Levellers had not supported manhood suffrage in the Putney debates and elsewhere since they wished to exclude servants, alms-takers and wage labourers from the electorate. Hill supported MacPherson.[83] Some historians have taken the MacPherson thesis as an admission that Marxists accept a view of the Levellers which diminishes their status as radicals. But this is not the case and the reason why not is illustrative of the Marxist understanding of the English Revolution. For Marxists, contrary to the stereotype, the revolutionaries of the English Revolution cannot be assimilated into a model developed to explain later working-class revolutions. These earlier movements, as Marx and Engels pointed out in the *Communist Manifesto*, are 'movements of minorities, or the inter-

[81] H. Shaw, *The Levellers* (London, Longman, 1968), p.97 and p.104.

[82] C. B. MacPherson, *The Political Theory of Possessive Individualism* (Oxford, OUP, 1962).

[83] See, for instance, Hill's early reaction to MacPherson in H N Brailsford, *The Levellers and the English Revolution*, p.694.

ests of minorities'.[84] They seek to supplant one ruling minority with another. To do so, they mobilise wider layers of the population, but there is no necessary link between their interests and those of the wider groups to which they appeal. So to find that the Levellers appealed beyond their ranks and beyond the bounds of their own class but not necessarily in universal terms would be a confirmation of this analysis - which was part of MacPherson's point.

Yet, as a matter of fact, MacPherson and Hill were wrong. Macpherson based his analysis on a few phrases of Maximilian Petty's in the Putney Debates and on only one of the three editions of the *Agreement of the People*. On most occasions and in general, the Levellers stuck by a wider view of who should be able to vote. Nevertheless, the reasons for the compromises are interesting. In both cases, at Putney and in the second *Agreement of the People*, the Levellers were interacting with wider political forces which they were trying to get to accept as many of their demands as possible. The compromises were aimed at sustaining the forward momentum of the revolution. To the extent that they did limit the franchise, it was because they thought that servants and alms-takers were under the sway of masters and not able to properly exercise their freedom of expression, especially since there were no secret ballots. The Levellers feared the conservative impact that this would have. Although this view is contested, it seems that to the extent that the Levellers are less than full democrats, it is only because they were more determined revolutionaries.[85]

---

[84] K. Marx and F. Engels, *The Communist Manifesto*, p.49.

[85] For some of the discussion on this issue see A. L. Morton, 'Leveller Democracy - Fact or Myth?' in *The World of the Ranters*; K. Thomas, 'The Levellers and the Franchise' in G. E. Aylmer (ed.) *The Interregnum, the Quest for a Settlement* (Basingstoke, MacMillan, 1972), pp.57-79; R. Howell, Jr. and D. E. Brewster, 'Reconsidering the Levellers: The Evidence of the Moderate'; J. C. Davis, 'The Levellers and Democracy', *Past and Present* No.40 (Jul. 1968) pp.174-80; C. Thompson, 'Maximilian Petty and the Putney Debate on the Franchise', *Past and Present* No. 88 (Aug. 1980), pp.63-9; B. Taft, 'The Council of Officers' Agreement of the People, 1648/9', *The Historical Journal* 28, No.1 (Mar. 1985), pp.169-85. Also see M. Goldsmith, 'Levelling by Sword, Spade and Word: Radical Egalitarianism in the English

Some of the characteristics of this debate - textual analysis at the expense of a wider social history, close study of individual moments at the expense of examining the longer social process, neglect of political dynamics - were signs of things to come.

IV

The revisionist challenge to liberal and left interpretations of the English Revolution synchronised with almost suspicious exactitude with the end of the post-war boom and the abandonment of the welfare-state consensus. This change, beginning in the mid-1970s, achieved its electoral representation when Margaret Thatcher became prime minister of Britain in 1979 and Ronald Reagan president of the US in 1980. One of the arguments made against the left by the revisionists was that they read their current political preoccupations back into history. But if that was sometimes true of the left, it was also certainly true of some revisionists. You can almost hear the snap of Gordon Gekko's red braces in the background as J. C. D. Clark quotes approvingly a letter to the *Times Educational Supplement*:

> 'British political science was particularly torpid until the electoral shock of 1979. Too many existing political scientists belong to the generation of 1968 - a provenance that almost disqualifies them from comment on late 20th century politics.'[86]

Clark was equally opposed to, in his words, the 'Old Hat' historians of the S. R. Gardiner school and the 'Old Guard' historians 'formed in the matrix of inter-war Marxism' and the 'Class of 68'.[87]

Revisionism drew on the work of, among others, Conrad Russell,

---

Revolution' in C. Jones, M. Newitt, S. Roberts (eds.), *Politics and People in Revolutionary England* (Oxford, 1986), pp.65-80.

86 Quoted in J. Rees, 'Revolution Denied' in L. German and R. Hoveman (eds.), *A Socialist Review* (London, Bookmarks, 1998), p.120. Gordon Gekko was the fictional corporate raider of Oliver Stone's 1987 film *Wall Street*.

87 J. C. D. Clark, *Revolution and Rebellion* (Cambridge, CUP, 1986), pp.21-3.

Mark Kishlansky, Kevin Sharpe, John Morrill, and Peter Laslett.[88] The major themes of revisionism were a stress on the accidental nature of the revolution rather than on its long-term social and economic causes; a localist denial of nationally operative causes of the revolution; an insistence that religious issues were more central to the revolution than previous historians had allowed; an attempt to deny that the revolution involved class conflict or that the mass of people had much impact on its outcome; a corresponding emphasis on 'high politics' as a key determinant of events. This is not the place in which all these general issues can be explored, but we can examine some of the arguments as they have been applied to the Levellers.[89] Two issues are of particular interest. One is the religious dimension of Leveller organisation, the second is the impact of the Levellers as a movement.

Murray Tolmie is by no means a stereotypical revisionist, but he is a critic of 'whig historians' and of A. L. Morton and Christopher Hill for neglecting the role of 'respectable nonconformity' and religious sects.[90] *The Triumph of the Saints* is a powerful act of historical recovery which substantially adds to our knowledge of the religious underground from which some of the Leveller leaders emerged. It shows that the Levellers learned a proto-democratic ideology in the Independent churches and that it gave them a history of oppo-

---

[88] C. Russell, *The Causes of the English Civil War* (Oxford, OUP, 1990); M. Kishlansky, 'The Army and the Levellers: the roads to Putney', *Historical Journal* 22 (1979), pp.795-824, 'Consensus Politics and the Structure of Debate at Putney', *Journal of British Studies* 20 (1981), pp.50-69, 'What happened at Ware?', *Historical Journal* 25 (1982), pp.827-39; J. Morrill, *The Revolt of the Provinces* (London, Longman, 1976), *The Nature of the English Revolution* (London, Longman, 1993); K. Sharpe, *The Personal Rule of Charles I* (New Haven, Yale, 1996); P. Laslett, *The World We Have Lost Further Explored* (London, Methuen, 1983). See also the summary revisionist case in A. MacLachlan, *The Rise and Fall of Revolutionary England.*

[89] I have attempted a brief reply to the revisionists in J Rees, 'Revolution Denied'.

[90] M. Tolmie, *The Triumph of the Saints, the Separate Churches of London 1616-1649* (Cambridge, CUP, 1977), pp.ix-x.

sitional organisation. Tolmie shows that the Levellers continued to rely on the gathered churches for organisational support until the crisis which saw them separate once and for all from their sometime Independent allies in the late 1640s.

But Tolmie's close reading of the development of these relations ends in a question that he fails adequately to answer: if the same religious and church organisation formed both the Levellers and their Independent competitors in the crisis of the late 1640s, what was it that caused the division? Similar formation led to divergent conclusions. Why? It is here that social and political factors must supplement purely religious explanations. Certainly, the Independents in the gathered churches did not like some of the religious ideas that, say, Walwyn or Overton, held. But there was more to it than that. There was political division over the programme that the Levellers had developed and which had had no part of their common history with the churches. It was new, born as a predominantly political response to the events of the revolution. And reinforcing this difference in politics was a social difference. In his *Merchants and Revolution*, Robert Brenner follows Tolmie's analysis, but puts it in a wider social frame, noting the connections between the leaders of the Independent churches and the new merchants that he sees as a decisive force in the revolution. Indeed, they are often the same people. He charts how the Independents broke from the Levellers precisely over the question of democracy, some retreating from reform in national politics to reform of London government where they had more at stake and more control.[91] Brenner's treatment of Tolmie's argument provides a model for the handling of the religious dimension of the English revolution.

And if the question of the religious affiliation of the Levellers has sometimes been neglected, it is also the case that it can be overstated. In his introduction to *The English Levellers* collection of texts, Andrew Sharpe suggests the Levellers' only justification for their arguments 'derived from one's Christian duty to seek and speak God's truth'. Sharpe ignores their appeals to the rights of free-born

---

[91] R. Brenner, *Merchants and Revolution* (Cambridge, CUP, 1993) p.533-41.

Englishmen, the Common Law and to the theory of the Norman Yoke, essentially secular arguments.[92] Rachel Foxley's 'John Lilburne and the Citizenship of "Free-Born Englishmen"' establishes by careful analysis of Lilburne's writings that he developed notions of a uniform and inclusive citizenship and of democratic rights that were independent of religious justifications.[93] Elsewhere Foxley argues:

> 'The standard view of the nature of the political society which the Levellers endorse is that it is a form of popular sovereignty - as distinct from the parliamentary sovereignty which some parliamentarians had already advocated. Scott speaks of the Levellers' key demand as "popular self-government through representatives".'[94]

Unlike Murray Tolmie, Mark Kishlansky is a representative revisionist figure. His 'The Army and the Levellers: The Roads to Putney' is a systematic attempt to reduce the role of the Levellers in the radicalisation of the army and therefore in the events which attend the peak of the revolution in the years 1647-1650.[95] The core of the argument is this: the rank and file of the army were mostly concerned with pay and disbandment, their political consciousness only grew slowly through this period and it had relatively little to

---

[92] A. Sharp (ed.), p.xix. G. E. Aylmer's introduction to his 1975 selection of Leveller writings is much more careful in its analysis. G. E. Aylmer (ed.), *The Levellers and the English Revolution.* See also the valuable account of Walwyn's life and ideas in J. R. Michael and B. Taft (eds.), *The Writings of William Walwyn* (Athens, University of Georgia Press, 1989), pp.1-51.
[93] R. Foxley, 'John Lilburne and the Citizenship of "Free-Born Englishmen"' in *The Historical Journal* 47, 4 (2004), pp.849–74.
[94] R. Foxley, 'Problems of Sovereignty in Leveller Writings', *History of Political Thought* XXVIII, No.4 (Winter 2007).
[95] M. Kishlansky, 'The Army and the Levellers: The Roads to Putney'. A similar approach is taken by John Morrill and Phillip Baker, 'The Case of the Armie Truly Re-stated' in M. Mendle (ed.), pp.103-24. But, as Rachel Foxley comments in her review of Mendle, this approach 'ultimately creates as many problems of interpretation as it solves'. See R. Foxley, 'John Lilburne and the Citizenship of "Free-Born Englishmen"', p.1010.

do with the Levellers. The army wanted unity and was resistant to the Levellers who they saw as divisive. In short: the military workers weren't political; they were deferential to their bosses and didn't want to be mixed up with 'outside agitators'.

Kishlansky has been contradicted in an effective manner by Austin Woolrych's account of the Putney Debates and the events surrounding them, *Soldiers and Statesmen*, and by Ian Gentles' work on the New Model Army and Norah Carlin's examination of the Levellers' organisation in London.[96] But, oddly, Kishlansky's actual account of events is much more Marxist, Leninist even, than he might be happy to acknowledge. Properly understood, a Marxist analysis of the relationship between an organised militant group and a wider mass during a revolutionary upheaval would be likely to stress the fact that, at the outset, the ideas of the minority and those of the mass will be at least partially opposed, but that under the impact of events, the radicalisation of the mass and the process of learning how to respond to this on the part of the organised minority raises the possibility of an effective political alliance. As part of this process, Levellers and elected agitators grew together - before Putney, at Putney, after Putney. Nor should the impulse for unity surprise us. The argument at Putney was an argument within the revolutionary camp. Such arguments are always disciplined by the relations between the revolutionary camp and counter-revolutionary forces. This is especially so when the conflict takes the form of civil war. One only has to think of the Spanish Civil War to see a related dynamic, especially in Barcelona. What Kishlansky thinks is an account which undermines a Marxist understanding of the revolutionary process actually tends to confirm it.

---

[96] Kishlansky's full account is available in his *The Rise of the New Model Army* (Cambridge, CUP, 1979). See also A. Woolrych, *Soldiers and Statesmen, The General Council of the Army and its Debates* (Oxford, OUP, 1987), I. Gentles, The New Model Army (Oxford, Balckwell, 1992), N. Carlin, 'Leveller Organization in London' in *The Historical Journal* 27, No.4 (Dec. 1984), pp. 955-60. See also N. Carlin, 'The Levellers and the Conquest of Ireland in 1649', *The Historical Journal* 30, No.2 (June, 1987), pp.269-88.

V

Revisionism was essentially a negative intellectual trend in the sense that its leading figures could find broad agreement on what they were against, but had no common account of the English Revolution that could replace those that they criticised. Localism, the accidental nature of the revolution, a return to the study of elite politics, a stress on the continuity of British history in the seventeenth century were elements that it was hard to combine in a convincing synthesis. As Mark Kishlansky declared in his overview of the revolution, *A Monarchy Transformed*, 'I believe that no synthesis of modern scholarship can result in a single, coherent, up-to-date narrative, and I have not chosen to provide one ... Beyond the opening chapter, there is nothing on social, economic or women's history; beyond the analytic discussion in Chapter 2, little on local history ... There is no treatment of intellectual life here - of literature, philosophy, science, or fine arts.'[97] Consequently *A Monarchy Transformed* is much less striking than Kishlansky's essays on the Levellers and the army.

In a way, revisionism was never only about the English Revolution. Very similar arguments were deployed at much the same time about the French and the Russian Revolutions. Moreover, the revisionists depended on a wider conservative turn in social theory. The Althusserian school of the 1970s, which became the post-structuralist school, which became the post-modernist school which fed the 'linguistic turn', provided a theoretical toolbox for the revisionists and those that came after them.[98]

One important effect of revisionism has been to marginalise an impressive body of work by Marxist historians. Even now it is common to focus on the work Christopher Hill to the exclusion of other work by Marxists. Brian Manning's imaginative reinterpreta-

---

[97] M Kishlansky, *A Monarchy Transformed*, pp.x-xi.

[98] For some critical accounts of these developments see E. P. Thompson, *The Poverty of Theory and Other Essays* (London, Merlin, 1978), pp.193-397, J. Rees, *The Algebra of Revolution*, pp.290-302, A. Callinicos, *Against Postmodernism* (Cambridge, Polity, 1989), C. Norris, *Uncritical Theory* (London, Lawrence and Wishart, 1992), M. O'Brien, 'Postmodernism and British History' in J. Rees (ed.), *Essays on Historical Materialism*, ch.6.

tion of the class analysis of the English revolution was developed across five major works beginning with *The English People and the English Revolution* (1976) and ending with *Revolution and Counter Revolution in England, Ireland and Scotland 1658-60* (2003).[99] Manning's work reached publication during the high tide of revisionism, with the result that it received limited attention and was too easily dismissed.[100] For Manning, the central political agency in the revolution was the 'middling sort', a contemporary term that Manning adopted to avoid revisionist charges of anachronism. This refurbished class analysis, significantly different from that in Hill's later work, allowed Manning to revisit the Levellers and to reaffirm their centrality to the events that determined the outcome of the revolution.

Robert Brenner's *Merchants and Revolution* was less concerned with agency in a narrow sense, but it did provide a long-term social and economic model of the revolution. Other work sympathetic to Brenner's approach, by Ellen Meiskins Wood and Neal Wood, dealt with ideology and the growth of capitalism in *A Trumpet of Sedition*. Norah Carlin provided a modern Marxist contribution to the debate about the causes of the revolution. James Holstun achieved the seemingly impossible task of directly confronting the postmodernists on their own theoretical ground while simultaneously providing an anti-revisionist history of radicalism in the revolution in *Ehud's Dagger*.[101] Some of the most interesting, detailed insights into the Levellers

---

[99] B. Manning, *The English People and the English Revolution, 1649, The Crisis of the English Revolution* (1992), *Aristocrats, Plebeians and Revolution in England 1640-1660* (London, Pluto Press, 1996), *The Far Left in the English Revolution 1640-1660* (London, Bookmarks, 1999), *Revolution and Counter Revolution in England Ireland and Scotland 1658-60* (London, Bookmarks, 2003)

[100] For one overview of the academic reception of Manning's work see I. Gentles, 'Soldiers, Levellers and the "Middle Sort" in the English Revolution', https://pi.library.yorku.ca/ojs/index.php/lh/article/viewFile/5253/4449

[101] E. Meiksins Wood and N. Wood, *The Trumpet of Sedition, Political Theory and the Rise of Capitalism 1509-1688* (London, Pluto Press, 1997), E. Meiksins Wood, *The Pristine Culture of Capitalism* (London,

have come from histories with a wider focus than the Levellers themselves, such as Keith Lindley's *Popular Politics and Religion in Civil War London*. Indeed, sometimes the focus has been on the enemies of the Levellers in, for instance, Robert Ashton's *Counter-Revolution* and Ann Hughes' study of Thomas Edwards' *Gangraena*.[102]

Both revisionism and post-modernism have now run their course, leaving behind scepticism of 'grand narratives' but no identifiable general theory (precisely because the theory was that there is no general theory). In their wake, the historians of the Levellers in the English Revolution have begun to produce some interesting work. Nicholas Tyacke has argued that, since the 1980s, 'a new group of historians has emerged, often collectively referred to as "post-revisionists"' whose work 'at least implicitly' incorporates insights from early Marxist and liberal interpretive models.[103] Ann Hughes produced a valuable non-revisionist account of the causes of the revolution in 1991.[104] In 2000, Sarah Barber produced the first full-length biography of Henry Marten, *A Revolutionary Rogue*. Barber eschews involvement in the wider controversies about the Levellers, but her valuable, straightforward account, like Marten's life and political history itself, could not be more at variance with the revisionist thesis.[105] Antonia Southern's *Forlorn Hope*, her account

---

Verso, 1991), N. Carlin, *The Causes of the English Civil War* (Oxford, Blackwell, 1999), J Holstun, *Ehud's Dagger: Class Struggle in the English Revolution* (London: Verso 2002).

[102] K. Lindley, *Popular Politics and Religion in Civil War London* (Aldershot, Scolar, 1997), R. Ashton, *Counter-Revolution, The Second Civil War and its Origins, 1646-8* (New Haven, Yale, 1994), A. Hughes, *Gangraena and The Struggle for the English Revolution* (Oxford, OUP, 2004).

[103] N. Tyacke, 'Introduction: locating the "English Revolution",' in N. Tyacke (ed.), *The English Revolution c.1590-1720*, pp.1-2.

[104] A. Hughes, *The Causes of the English Civil War* (Basingstoke, MacMillan, 1991).

[105] S. Barber, *A Revolutionary Rogue, Henry Marten and the English Republic* (Stroud, Sutton, 2000). Though not about the Levellers, Geoffrey Robertson's account of the life of John Cook in his *The Tyrannicide Brief, The Story of the Man who sent Charles I to the Scaffold* (London,

of the lives of five leading Levellers, has many of the same virtues.[106] More recently, David Como's work of historical reconstruction has resulted in the attribution to William Walwyn of a pamphlet whose authorship was previously unknown. And more generally, his 'Secret Printing, the Crisis of 1640 and the Origins of Civil War Radicalism' has opened a window on the early formation of the Levellers. This is an important contribution to an area of study too long neglected and, taken together with Tolmie's work, begins to give us the elements of a pre-history of the Leveller movement.[107]

Rachel Foxley's recent work has culminated in her *The Levellers, Radical Thought in the English Revolution* which consistently undermines much of the revisionist case against the Levellers, focussing on their contribution to the ideological ferment of the revolutionary decades.[108] Jason Peacey has contributed a careful survey of the way in which the opponents of the Levellers used their own printing presses to respond to the Levellers' pamphlet campaigns. His work shows that the Levellers and their Presbyterian and Independent rivals developed a certain symmetry of method if not of aim in addressing the audience awakened to political debate by the revolution. In another article, 'John Lilburne and the Long Parliament', Peacey traces the connections between Lilburne and his 'powerful friends at Westminster'. Peacey attributes some of Lilburne's difficulties to rivalries at Westminster rather than to his radical ideas. This is a valuable reminder of how fluid the social structure can become in revolution. But we should be careful not to remain within a binary explanation of Lilburne's predicament - either it was his

---

Chatto and Windus, 2005) ploughs a similarly engaging furrow.

[106] A. Southern, *Forlorn Hope, Soldier Radicals of the Seventeenth Century* (Lewes, The Book Guild, 2001).

[107] D. Como, 'An Unattributed Pamphlet by William Walwyn: New Light on the Prehistory of the Leveller Movement' in *The Huntington Library Quarterly*; 2006; 69, 3 and 'Secret Printing, The Crisis of 1640, and the Origins of Civil War Radicalism' in Past and Present 196 (August 2007).

[108] R. Foxley, *The Levellers, Radical Thought in the English Revolution* (Manchester, MUP, 2013). For my longer assessment of Foxley's book see the Institute of Historical Research, Reviews in History: http://www.history.ac.uk/reviews/review/1519

ideas or elite rivalry that caused the problems he faced. We should consider the fact that it might have been the unique organisational form that embodied Leveller ideas, as well as the ideas themselves, which made Lilburne a threatening figure.[109]

The post-revisionist wave really became much more powerful after the publication of Rachel Foxley's *The Levellers* in 2013. The same year, John Donoghue's *Fire Under the Ashes* looked at radical links across the Atlantic. Elliot Vernon is right to say that 'the field of study is currently buzzing with new scholarship', and it is now difficult to keep abreast of the really excellent work being published. Gary De Krey published two volumes of *Following the Levellers* in 2018 which contributed much specialised detail of the movement and, especially, charted its continuing influence into the 1650s. The same year, *John Lilburne and the Levellers* collected a series of essays from leading historians including Ann Hughes, Jason Peacey, and Ted Vallance that had originated as papers given at the Lilburne 400 conference in 2015. Again in 2018, Michael Braddick produced *The Common Freedom of the People, John Lilburne and the English Revolution*, the first biography of Lilburne since Pauline Gregg's *Free-born John* in 1961. And David Como rounded out a bonanza year with his pathbreaking *Radical Parliamentarians*, charting the relationship of parliamentarian activists, including Levellers, with the wider course of the English revolution. In 2020, Norah Carlin's long-awaited research on petitioning by radicals in the crucial years of 1648-1649, *Regicide or Revolution?* was published. Jordan Downs, *Civil War London*, appeared in 2021 and gave a new and graphic account of popular mobilisation in the capital during the Civil War years. The following year Michael Sturza produced *The London Revolution, 1640-1643* which gave a broader and explicitly Marxist take on the same phenomena.[110]

---

[109] J. Peacey, 'The hunting of the Leveller: the sophistication of parliamentarian propaganda, 1647–53', *Historical Research* 78, No.199 (February 2005) and 'John Lilburne and the Long Parliament', *The Historical Journal* 43, No.3 (Sep. 2000). This last can usefully be read alongside G. E. Aylmer, 'Gentlemen Levellers?', pp.120-5.

[110] E. Vernon, review of *Following the Levellers*, (review no. 2350), DOI: 10.14296/RiH/2014/2350, Date accessed: 12 June 2023. Recent

VI

The transmission of the history of the Levellers through the generations since the seventeenth century has been an uneven and discontinuous process. We can identify three major factors affecting how this history has been understood.

The first is the political environment in each succeeding phase of social development, including the strength and nature of radical currents within society. From the Restoration to the rise of neoliberalism (and its academic correlates) there have been times when the Levellers were seen as unacceptable politically or unimportant historically. There have also been times, the early nineteenth-century birth of the workers movement, the late nineteenth-century apex of liberal progressivism, the 1940s to the 1970s, when the broader social and political environment seemed more conducive to recovering Leveller history and proclaiming its importance.

Secondly, the experience of subsequent revolutionary eruptions, especially the American and French revolutions, the European Revolutions of 1848 and the Russian Revolution, impact on our understanding of previous revolutions. But this impact is always mediated. The effect of the Russian Revolution in Britain, for instance,

---

important work on the Levellers and related areas of research includes, E. Vernon and P. Baker, *The Agreements of the People, The Levellers, and the Constitutional Crisis of the English Revolution*. R. Foxley, *The Levellers, Radical Political Thought in the English Revolution),* G. De Krey, *Following the Levellers*, Vol. I (London, Palgrave Macmillan, 2017). G. De Krey, *Following the Levellers*, Vol. II (London, Palgrave Macmillan, 2018). J. Rees (ed.), *John Lilburne and the Levellers* (London, Routledge, 2018). M. Braddick, *The Common Freedom of the People, John Lilburne and the English Revolution* (Oxford, OUP, 2018). D. Como, *Radical Parliamentarians* (Oxford, OUP, 2018). N. Carlin, *Regicide or Revolution?* J. Donoghue, *Fire Under the Ashes* (Chicago, Chicago University Press, 2013). J. S. Downs, *Civil War London* (Manchester, MUP, 2021). M. Sturza, *The London Revolution, 1640-1643*. See also R. Bell, 'Print networks, manuscript pamphleteering, and the development of prison politics in seventeenth-century London', *Journal of British Studies* (CUP, 2023), pp.1-33.

was mediated first by the crisis of the 1920s and 1930s, the rise of fascism and the Second World War. It was mediated again by the political forces - liberal, left Labour and Communist Party - that recovered the Leveller history for the twentieth century. And it was mediated a third time by the precise dispositions of the individual authors within this matrix. Increasingly, from the 1950s onwards, the character of academic discussion in newly expanded universities has shaped what is said about the Levellers. This has important advantages over narrowly instrumental political history of the Whig and Tory variety. But the academy also tends to de-politicise and compartmentalise in a way which is unhelpful in the study of dynamic, society-wide social upheavals.

Finally, the condition of historical knowledge and the degree to which this knowledge is widely known in any given period configures our understanding of the Levellers. Perhaps this is the most under-examined element in understanding the historical reception of Leveller history. There can be no tradition and no debate where there is no knowledge. That is why the discovery of the *Clarke Papers* and the publication of the Leveller tracts in the 1940s mark turning points in the reception of the Levellers every bit as much as wider social developments.

Conclusion

Christopher Hill included in his introduction to *The Crisis of the Seventeenth Century* six points that he thought captured the common ground among the historians who contributed to that collection and, perhaps, by extension, a wider community of seventeenth-century scholars.[1]

Hill's points amounted to this: that there was a general economic and political crisis in Europe in the seventeenth century and that comparisons across the continent were the nearest historians could get to a 'laboratory test' that might reveal the causes of those events. That these crises differed according to the social and political structures and religious institutions and beliefs in the various nations effected. That the outcome of this crisis was markedly different in England and the Netherlands, 'where political revolutions led to significant economic and social changes', than it was in other European countries. That the revolution in Britain could be illuminated by comparing it with the 'abortive revolts' in France, Spain and Italy.

The essays in the book seemed to confirm Hill's view. Hugh Trevor Roper, for instance, took Marxism seriously in his critique and perhaps adopted rather more of its substantive propositions in his analysis than he realised. All the essays shared a view that there were long-term causes of the revolutions across Europe, that they were not the result of a series of accidents, and that socio-economic factors had an important place among those causes.[2]

The post-revisionist moment is perhaps only now beginning to reconsider the English revolution in this kind of framework. The revisionist emphasis on accident, on short-term factors, on localism, and on elite politics maybe behind us, but we have not yet seen many attempts to provide a longer-term account of the causes of the English Revolution and even fewer attempts to locate socio-economic drivers of the revolution.

---

[1] C. Hill, 'Introduction', T. H. Aston (ed.), *Crisis in Europe 1560-1660* (London, RKP, 1965), p.3.

[2] H. R. Trevor-Roper, 'The General Crisis of the Seventeenth Century', T. H. Aston (ed.), *Crisis in Europe 1560-1660*, pp.65-72.

This book has sought to reexamine why such long-term causes are worthy of investigation if we are to make any sense of the comparative evidence of popular revolution in Europe in the mid-seventeenth century. It has tried to clear away some misconceptions about Marxism and attempted to show ways in which class analysis properly deployed can help illuminate what the English people did between 1640 and 1660, and why they did it.

None of this should be taken to mean a simple return to previous debates. That is not desirable and it is just not possible. In any case, some of those debates were simply misconceived. The so-called 'storm over the gentry' is a good example. To try to tie the question of agency in the revolution too closely to a section of the gentry, whether the gentry faced with relative impoverishment or the rising gentry benefitting from new market-oriented production, is too linear an approach. That market-oriented methods of production and management were growing in both town and country in England in the seventeenth century is not in doubt. But this was a society-wide economic transformation with society-wide social and cultural changes attendant upon it. Any given individual did not have to be directly affected by it as an immediate economic experience to relate to the change that was all around.

One might be sympathetic to a religious transformation, like the growth of Puritanism, whether or not one was an improving landlord. One might be a middling-sort advocate of free trade, as many Levellers were, in spite of the fact that free trade was ultimately the undoing of many of the middle sort.

The ways in which economic transformations are reflected in political agency are sometimes direct, often not, and frequently contradictory. But what this fact demands of historians is not the abandonment of the link between economy and society, but a closer and more flexible approach which reflects the full complexity of the relationships.

It was not for nothing that although Marx famously developed a two-class model of capitalism in his economic theory, when it came to historical or political analysis his writings record much more numerous interacting classes and fractions of classes. In *The Class Struggles in France*, for example, Marx mentions the bourgeoise, the republican bourgeoisie, the financial aristocracy, the industrial bourgeoisie, the petite bourgeoise, the republican petite bourgeoise, the middle classes, big landed property, the peasant class, the working class, and the lumpenproletariat, as well as 'the *ideological* spokesmen of the classes mentioned, their scholars, lawyers, doctors etc., in a word, their so-called *authorities*'.[3]

It has been the simple aim of this book to suggest that a more informed engagement with this tradition, rather than a causal dismissal of it, will enhance, as it has done in the past, our understanding of the English Revolution.

---

[3] K. Marx, The Class Struggles in France in K. Marx, *Surveys from Exile* (London, Penguin, 1973), pp.35-45, 88, 101.

Bibliography

Primary

Behn, Aphra, *Oroonoko and other stories* (Koln, Konemann, 1999).
Burton, T., *Diary of Thomas Burton, Esq. Member in the Parliaments of Richard and Oliver Cromwell, From 1656 to 1659*, edited by John Towill Rutt (London, Henry Colburn, 1828).
Clarke, William, *The Clarke Papers*, ed. and intro. C. H. Firth (London, Royal Historical Society, 1992).
Cook, J., *King Charls his Case* (London, 1649), C6025 (Wing).
CSPD: Interregnum, 1654 (London, 1880).
CSPD: Interregnum, 1657-8 (London, 1884).
Declaration of the Commons of England (London, 1648), E528 [23].
Freize, J. *The Levellers Vindication…* (London, 1649), E573[8].
A Full Answer to the Levellers Petition (19 September 1648) Wing F2343.
Goodwin, J., *Hybristodkai, The Obstuctours of Justice* (London, 1649), E.572[2].
HMC, 'The manuscripts of Capt. F.C. Loder-Symonds', in *The Manuscripts of Rye and Hereford Corporations, etc. Thirteenth Report, Appendix: Part IV* (London, 1892).
The Humble Petition of divers well-affected Persons (London, 1668), E464[5].
King. *Two Tracts by Gregory King*, ed. G. E. Barnett (Baltimore, John Hopkins Press, 1936).
A Letter Sent form Newport (1648), E464 [29].
Ludlow, E., *The Memoirs of Edmund Ludlow*, Vol. I (Oxford, Clarendon Press, 1894).
Milton, J. *The Tenure of Kings and Magistrates* in S. Orgel and J. Goldberg (eds.), *John Milton* (Oxford, OUP, 1991).
Mercurius Politicus.
The Moderate.
The mournfull Cryes of many thousand poor tradesman, who are ready to famish through decay of Trade in D. Wolfe, *Leveller Manifestoes of the Puritan Revolution* (Frank Cass 1967).
New Engagement, or, Manifesto of 1648 (noted as collected August 3rd), N634 (Wing)
Nicholas. *The Nicholas Papers*, ed. G. F. Warner (London, Camden Society, 1897).
Orwell and Reynolds. *British Pamphleteers, Vol.1, From the Sixteenth Century to the French Revolution* (London: Allan Wingate 1948).
The Rebellion of Naples or the Tragedy of Massenello (London, 1649), B199 (Wing).
Roberts, S. K. (ed.), *The Cromwell Association Online Directory of Parliamentarian Army Officers* (2017).

Thurloe. *State Papers of John Thurloe, Vol. 6, January 1657 - March 1658* (London, 1742).
To the Honourable House of Commons… (London, 1641), Wing T1437.
A True Relation of the reducing of the The City of Naples To the Obedience of the King of Spaine (London, 1648), E438 [18].
Verity, V., *The Royal Project* (London, 1648), E468 [22].
A view of part of the many Traiterous, Disloyal and Turn-about Actions of H. H. Senior (1684), Wing (CD-Rom), V359.
Walwyn. *Gold Tried by Fire* in J. R. McMichael and B Taft, *The Writings of William Walwyn* (Athens and London, Georgia, 1989), pp.283-5.
Walwyn. *The Writings of William Walwyn*, eds. J. R. Michael and B. Taft (Athens, University of Georgia Press, 1989).
Wood, A. *Athenae Oxonienses, An Exact History of all the Writers and Bishops who have had their education at the most antient and famous University of Oxford* (London, R Knaplock, D. Midwinter and J. Tonson, MDCCXXI), Vol. II.

Secondary

Althusser, L. 'Contradiction and Overdetermination', *New Left Review* 41 (Jan/Feb 1967).
Anderson, P. *Lineages of the Absolutist State* (London, Verso, 1974).
------------, *Considerations on Western Marxism* (London, Verso edition, 1979).
Ashley, M. *John Wildman, Plotter and Postmaster, A study of the English Republican Movement in the Seventeenth Century* (London, Jonathan Cape, 1947).
Ashman, S. 'The Communist Party Historians' Group' in J. Rees (ed.), *Essays on Historical Materialism* (London, Bookmarks, 1998).
Ashton, R. *Counter-Revolution, The Second Civil War and its Origins, 1646-8* (New Haven, Yale, 1994).
Aston, T. H. (ed.), *Crisis in Europe 1560-1660* (London, RKP, 1965).
Aston, T. H. and Philpin, C. H. E. (eds.), *The Brenner Debate*, (Cambridge, CUP, 1985).
Aylmer, G. E. 'Gentlemen Levellers?', *Past and Present*, No.49 (Nov. 1970).
Aylmer, G. (ed.), *The Levellers and the English Revolution* (London, Thames and Hudson, 1975).
Baker, P. 'The Franchise Debate Revisited: the Levellers and the Army', in S. Taylor and G. Tapsell, *The Nature of the English Revolution Revisited* (Woodbridge, Boydell and Brewer, 2013).
Baker, P. and Vernon, E., (eds), *The Agreements of the People, the Levellers and the constitutional crisis of the English revolution.* (Basingstoke, Palgrave Macmillan, 2012).
Barber, S., *A Revolutionary Rogue, Henry Marten and the English Republic* (Stroud, Sutton, 2000).

Bell, R., 'Dens of Tyranny and Oppression: the Politics of Imprisonment in Seventeenth-Century London' (PhD dissertation, Stanford University, 2017).

--------- 'Print networks, manuscript pamphleteering, and the development of prison politics in seventeenth-century London', *Journal of British Studies* (CUP, 2023), pp.1-33.

Berens, L. H., *The Digger Movement in the Days of the Commonwealth* (Monmouth, Merlin, 2007).

Bernstein, E., *Cromwell and Communism* (Nottingham, Spokesman, 1980).

Boerio, D., 'The "Trouble in Naples" in the Political Information Arena of the English Revolution', in J. Raymond and N. Moxham, *News Networks in Early Modern Europe* (Leiden, Brill, 2016).

Bounds, P., 'Orwell and Englishness: The Dialogue with British Marxism', *Cultural Logic, An Electronic Journal of Marxist Theory and Practice* (2007) at http://clogic.eserver.org.

Braddick, M., *The Common Freedom of the People, John Lilburne and the English Revolution* (Oxford, OUP, 2018).

Braddick, M. J. and Withington, P., *Popular Culture and Political Agency in Early Modern England and Ireland* (Woodbridge, Boydell, 2017).

Brailsford, H. N., *The Levellers and the English Revolution, ed. Christopher Hill* (Nottingham, Spokesman, 1961).

Brandon, P., *War, Capital, and the Dutch State* (1588-1795) (Chicago, Haymarket, 2016).

Branson, N. and Heinemann, M., *Britain in the Nineteen Thirties* (St. Albans, Panther, 1973).

Brenner, R. *Merchants and revolution* (Cambridge, CUP, 1993).

Brockway, Fenner, *Britain's First Socialists* (London, Quartet, 1980).

Brogan, H., *Longman History of the United States of America* (London, Longman, 1985).

Brunton, D. and Pennington D. H., *Members of the Long Parliament* (London, George Allen & Unwin, 1954).

Burgess, G., 'On Revisionism: An Analysis of Early Stuart Historiography in the 1970s and 1980s', *The Historical Journal*, Vol.33, No.3 (Sep., 1990).

Callinicos, A., *Against Postmodernism* (Cambridge, Polity, 1989).

-------------- 'The Limits of "Political Marxism"', *New Left Review* 184 (Nov-Dec. 1990), pp.110-15.

--------------'England's Transition to Capitalism', *New Left Review*, 207 (Sept.-Oct. 1994) pp.124-133.

Caricchio, M., Tarantino G., eds., *Cromohs Virtual Seminars. Recent historiographical trends of the British Studies (17th-18th Centuries)*, 2006-2007.

Carlin, Norah, 'Marxism and the English Civil War', *International Socialism*, No.10 (1980).

----------------- 'Leveller Organization in London' in *The Historical Journal*, Vol.27, No.4 (Dec. 1984).
----------------- 'The Levellers and the Conquest of Ireland in 1649', *The Historical Journal*, Vol.30, No.2 (June 1987), pp.269-88.
---------------- *The Causes of the English Civil War* (Oxford, Blackwell, 1999).
---------------- *Regicide or Revolution? What Petitioners Wanted, September 1648-February 1649* (London, Breviary Stuff Press, 2020).
Challinor, R., *The Origins of British Bolshevism* (London, Croom Helm, 1977).
Clark, J. C. D., *Revolution and Rebellion* (Cambridge, CUP, 1986).
Cohen, G. A., *Karl Marx's Theory of History: A Defense* (Oxford University Press 1978).
Como, D., *Radical Parliamentarians* (Oxford, OUP, 2018).
------------ 'An Unattributed Pamphlet by William Walwyn: New Light on the Prehistory of the Leveller Movement' in *The Huntington Library Quarterly* 69, no.3 (2006).
------------ 'Secret Printing, The Crisis of 1640, and the Origins of Civil War Radicalism' in *Past and Present*, No.196 (August 2007).
Curelly, L., '"The French, those Monkies of Mankind": the Fronde as seen by the newsbook *Mercurius Politicus*', *XVII-XVIII: Revue de la Société d'études anglo-américaines des XVIIe et SVIII^e siècles* 69 (2012).
------------ '"Do look on the other side of the water": Cromwell's foreign policy towards France', *Revue Électronique D'Études sur le Monde Anglophone*, [Online], 11.2 | 2014, posted online on July 15, 2014, consulted on April 22, 2024. URL: http://journals.openedition.org/erea/3751
Curelly, L. and Smith N., Introduction, to L. Curelly and N. Smith (eds.), *Radical Voices, Radical Ways* (Manchester, MUP, 2016).
Davis, J. C., 'The Levellers and Democracy', Past and Present, No. 40 (Jul. 1968) pp. 174-180.
De Krey, G., *Following the Levellers*, 2 Vols. (London, Palgrave Macmillan, 2017/18).
Donnelly, F. K., 'Levellerism in Eighteenth and Early Nineteenth-Century Britain', *Albion* 20, 2 (Summer 1988).
Donoghue, J., *Fire Under the Ashes* (Chicago, Chicago University Press, 2013).
Downs, J. S., *Civil War London* (Manchester, MUP, 2021).
Draper, H., *Karl Marx's Theory of Revolution*, Vol. II, The Politics of Social Classes (New York and London, Monthly Review, 1978).
Eales, J., 'Alan Everitt and The Community of Kent revisited', in J. Eales, and A. Hopper eds., *County Community in Seventeenth Century England and Wales* (Hatfield, University of Hertfordshire Press, 2012).
Eales, J., and Hopper A. eds., *County Community in Seventeenth Century England and Wales* (Hatfield, University of Hertfordshire Press, 2012).
Earle, P., *The Making of the English Middle Class* (London: Methuen Publishing Ltd, 1989).

Eaude, M., *A People's History of Catalonia* (London, Pluto, 2022).
Elliott, J. H., *The Revolt of the Catalans, A Study in the Decline of Spain 1598-1640* (Cambridge, CUP, 1963).
-------------, 'Revolts in the Spanish Monarchy' in R. Forster and J. P. Greene, *Preconditions of Revolution in Early Modern Europe* (Baltimore, John Hopkins Press, 1970).
Engels, F. [and K. Marx], *Revolution and Counter-Revolution in Germany* (London, Lawrence and Wishart, 1933).
----------- 'The Position of England, The Eighteenth Century' in K Marx and F Engels, *Articles on Britain* (Moscow, Progress, 1975).
----------- *Anti-Duhring* (Peking, Foreign Languages Press, 1976).
----------- *The Peasant War in Germany* (Moscow, Progress, 1977).
----------- *Socialism Utopian and Scientific* (London, Bookmarks, 1993).
----------- 'Introduction to The Class Struggles in France' (1895) in K. Marx, *The Class Struggles in France* (Chippendale NSW, Resistance Books, 2003).
Everitt, Alan, *The Community of Kent and the Great Rebellion, 1640-60* (Leicester, Leicester University Press, 1966).
Firth, C. H., 'Thomas Scot's Account of his Actions as Intelligencer during the Commonwealth', *English Historical Review*, Vol. XII, Issue XLV (Jan. 1897).
Foxley, R., 'John Lilburne and the Citizenship of "Free-Born Englishmen"' in *The Historical Journal*, 47, 4 (2004), pp.849–74.
------------ 'Problems of Sovereignty in Leveller Writings', *History of Political Thought*, Vol. XXVIII. No.4 (Winter 2007).
------------ *The Levellers, Radical Thought in the English Revolution* (Manchester, MUP, 2013).
Frank. *The Levellers, A History of the Writings of Three Seventeenth Century Social Democrats John Lilburne, Richard Overton, William Walwyn* (1955).
Fulbrook, M., 'The English Revolution and the Revisionist Revolt', *Social History*, Vol.7, No.3 (Oct. 1982).
Gardiner, S. R., *History of the Great Civil War* (Witney: Windrush Press 1987).
----------------- *History of the Commonwealth and Protectorate* (Witney: Windrush Press 1988).
Gentles, I., *The New Model Army* (Oxford, Balckwell, 1992).
------------ 'Soldiers, Levellers and the "Middle Sort" in the English Revolution', *Left History: An Interdisciplinary Journal of Historical Inquiry and Debate* 2, no.1 (1994).
------------ 'Soldiers, Levellers and the "Middle Sort" in the English Revolution', https://pi.library.yorku.ca/ojs/index.php/lh/article/viewFile/5253/4449
German, L. and Hoveman, R. (eds.) *A Socialist Review* (London, Bookmarks, 1998).
Gibb, M. A., *John Lilburne The Leveller, A Christian Democrat* (London, Lindsay Drummond, 1947).

Goldsmith, M., 'Levelling by Sword, Spade and Word: Radical Egalitarianism in the English Revolution' in C. Jones, M. Newitt, S. Roberts (eds.), *Politics and People in Revolutionary England* (Oxford, 1986), pp.65-80.
Gooch, G. P., *The History of English Democratic Ideas in the Seventeenth Century* (Cambridge, 1898).
Gregg, P., *Free-Born John* (London, Dent, 1961).
Gurney, J., *Gerrard Winstanley* (London, Pluto, 2013).
Harris, T., 'The Leveller Legacy: from Restoration to the Exclusion Crisis' in M Mendle (ed.), *The Putney Debates of 1647, the army the levellers and the English state* (Cambridge, CUP, 2001)
-----------, 'Revisiting the Causes of the English Civil War', *Huntington Library Quarterly*, vol.78 no.4 (2015) pp. 615-35.
Healey, J., *The Blazing World* (London, Bloomsbury, 2023).
Heller, H., *The Birth of Capitalism* (Halifax, NS, Fernwood, 2011).
Hessayon, A., 'Fabricating radical traditions', in M. Caricchio, G. Tarantino, eds., *Cromohs Virtual Seminars. Recent historiographical trends of the British Studies (17th-18th Centuries)*, 2006-2007.
Hessayon, A. and Finnegan, D. (eds.), *Varieties of Seventeenth- and Early Eighteenth-Century Radicalism in Context* (Farnham, Ashgate, 2011).
Hill, C., 'Soviet Interpretations of the English Interregnum', *Economic History Review*, No.8 (1938), pp.159-67.
-------------------- 'The English Civil War Interpreted by Marx and Engels, *Science and Society*, Vol.12. No.1 (Winter 1948).
-------------------- *The Century of Revolution 1603-1714* (Wokingham, Van Nostrand, Reinhold, 1961.
-------------------- 'Introduction', T. H. Aston (ed.), *Crisis in Europe 1560-1660* (London, RKP, 1965), p.3.
-------------------- *Reformation of Industrial Revolution* (London, Pelican, 1967).
-------------------- *God's Englishman* (London, Pelican, 1970).
-------------------- 'Parliament and People in Seventeenth-Century England: A Rejoinder', *Past & Present*, No.98 (Feb. 1983).
-------------------- *The Experience of Defeat, Milton and Some Contemporaries* (London, Faber, 1984).
-------------------- 'Radical Pirates?' in *Collected Essays*, vol.3 (Brighton, Harvester 1986).
-------------------- 'The Poor and the People in Seventeenth-Century England' in F. Krantz (ed.), *History From Below* (Oxford, Blackwell, 1988) pp.29-53.
-------------------- in L. Humber and J. Rees, 'The Good Old Cause - an interview with Christopher Hill, *International Socialism* 56 (London, 1992).
Hill, C. and Dell E. (eds.), *The Good Old Cause, The English Revolution of 1640-1660, Its Causes, Courses and Consequences* (London, Frank Cass, 1949).
Hill, C., James M., Rickword, E., *Three Essays in Interpretation, The English Revolution 1640* (London, Lawrence and Wishart, 1940).

Hobsbawm, E., 'The General Crisis of the European Economy in the 17th Century', *Past & Present*, No.5, (May 1954).

---------------- 'The Historians' Group of the Communist Party' in *Rebels and their Causes: Essays in Honour of A. L. Morton* (London, Lawrence and Wishart, 1978), pp.21–47.

---------------- *The Age of Extremes* (London, Michael Joseph, 1994).

Holmes, C., 'Review of The English People and the English Revolution by Brian Manning', in *The American Historical Review*, Vol.82, No.1 (Feb. 1977), pp.96-7.

------------- 'The county community in Stuart historiography' *Journal of British Studies*, Vol.19, No.2 (1980).

Holstun, J., *Ehud's Dagger: Class Struggle in the English Revolution* (London: Verso 2002).

Howell, R. Jr. and Brewster D. E., 'Reconsidering the Levellers: The Evidence of the Moderate', *Past and Present*, no.46 (Feb. 1970), pp.68-86.

Hudson, W. S., review, *Church History*, Vol.14, No.2 (Jun. 1945), pp.132-3.

Hudson, W., 'Economic and Social Thought of Gerrard Winstanley: Was he a Seventeenth Century Marxist?' in *The Journal of Modern History*, Vol.18, No.1, (March 1946) pp.1-21.

Hughes, A. *Politics, Society and Civil War in Warwickshire, 1620-1660* (Cambridge, CUP, 1987).

--------------- *The Causes of the English Civil War* (Basingstoke, MacMillan, 1991).

---------------- *Gangraena and The Struggle for the English Revolution* (Oxford, OUP, 2004).

Humber, L. and Rees, J., 'The Good Old Cause - an interview with Christopher Hill', *International Socialism* 56 (London, 1992).

Holstun, J., *Ehud's Dagger: Class Struggle in the English Revolution* (London, Verso Books, 2000).

James, C. L. R. (writing as G.F. Eckstein), 'Ancestors of the Proletariat' in *Fourth International*, Vol.10 No.8, September 1949.

------------------ 'Cromwell and the Levellers', *Fourth International*, Vol.10, No.5, May 1949, pp.143-148.

Jones, C., Newitt, M., Roberts, S. (eds.), *Politics and People in Revolutionary England* (Oxford, 1986).

Kaye, H., *The British Marxist Historians* (Cambridge, Polity, 1995).

Kelsey, S., 'The Trial of Charles I', *The English Historical Review*, Vol.118, No.477 (June 2003).

Kennedy, G., Freemen, *Free Labor, and Republican Discourses of Liberty in Early Modern England* https://www.academia.edu/1828606/Freemen_Free_Labour_and_Republican_Discourses_of_Liberty_in_Early_Modern_England?auto=download

Kishlansky, M., 'The Army and the Levellers: the roads to Putney', *Historical Journal* 22 (1979), pp.795-824.

------------------ *The Rise of the New Model Army* (Cambridge, CUP, 1979).
------------------ 'Consensus Politics and the Structure of Debate at Putney', *Journal of British Studies* 20 (1981), pp.50-69.
------------------ 'What happened at Ware?', *Historical Journal* 25 (1982), pp.827-39.
Knachbel, P. A., *England and the Fronde, The Impact of the English Civil War and Revolution in France* (New York, Cornell University Press, 1967).
Koenigsberger, H. G., 'The Revolt of Palermo in 1647', *The Cambridge Historical Journal*, Vol.8, No.3 (1946).
Kolakowski, K., *Main Currents of Marxism* (Oxford, OUP, 1978).
Lake, P. and Peacey, J., 'Introduction: rethinking public politics in the English Revolution' in P. Lake and J. Peacey (eds.), *Insolent Proceedings, Rethinking public politics in the English Revolution* (Manchester, MUP, 2022).
-------------------------- *Insolent Proceedings, Rethinking public politics in the English Revolution* (Manchester, MUP, 2022).
Larrain, J., *A Reconstruction of Historical Materialism* (London, Allen and Unwin, 1986).
Laslett, P., *The World We Have Lost Further Explored* (London, Methuen, 1983).
Lawson, D. F., '"Upon a Dangerous Design", The Career of Edward Sexby, 1647-1657' (PhD. thesis, University of Alabama, 2016).
Levine, B., Brier, S., Brundage, D., Countryman, E., Fennell, D., Rediker, M., *Who Built America? Working People and the Nation's Economy, Politics, Culture and Society*, Vol. I, (New York, Pantheon, 1989).
Lindert, P. H. and Williamson, J. G., 'Revising England's Social Tables 1688-1812', *Explorations in Economic History* 19 (1982).
Lindley, K., *Popular Politics and Religion in Civil War London* (Aldershot, Scolar, 1997).
Lukács, G., *History and Class Consciousness* (London, Merlin, 1971).
MacLachlan, A., *The Rise and Fall of Revolutionary England* (Basingstoke, Macmillan, 1996).
MacPherson, C. B., *The Political Theory of Possessive Individualism* (Oxford, OUP, 1962).
Manning, B., 'The Long Parliament and the English Revolution', *Past & Present*, No.5 (May 1954).
-------------- 'Class and the English Revolution', *International Socialism*, No.38 (Spring 1988).
-------------- *The English People and the English Revolution*, (originally published in 1976, 2nd edition, London, Bookmarks, 1991).
-------------- *1649, The Crisis of the English Revolution* (London, Bookmarks, 1992).
-------------- 'God, Hill, and Marx', *International Socialism*, No.59 (Summer 1993), pp.75-97.
-------------- *Aristocrats, Plebeians and Revolution in England, 1640-1660*

(London, Pluto, 1996).
--------------- *The Far Left and the English Revolution* (London, Bookmarks, 1999).
-------------- *Revolution and counter-revolution in England, Ireland, and Scotland, 1658-1660* (London, Bookmarks, 2003).
Manning, B. and Pennington, D., 'The Long Parliament', *Past & Present*, No.6 (Nov. 1954).
Marx, K., 'Marx to Friedrich Adolph Sorge in Hoboken' in K Marx and F Engels, *Selected Correspondence* (Moscow, Progress, 1955), pp.322-3.
----------'A Review of Guizot's Book, "Why Has The English Revolution Been Successful?"' in K Marx and F Engels, *Articles on Britain* (London: Lawrence & Wishart Ltd 1971).
---------- 'A Meeting' in Karl Marx and Frederick Engels, *Articles on Britain*, (London: Lawrence & Wishart Ltd 1971).
---------- The Class Struggles in France in K. Marx, *Surveys from Exile* (London, Penguin, 1973).
---------- 'Review of Guizot's Book on the English Revolution', in *Surveys from Exile* (London, Penguin, 1973).
---------- 'Theses of Feuerbach' in *Early Writings* (London, Penguin, 1974) pp.421-4.
---------- 'Moralising Criticism and Critical Morality' in Karl Marx and Frederick Engels, *MECW*, Vol.6 (London, Lawrence and Wishart, 1976).
---------- *The Class Struggles in France* (Chippendale NSW, Resistance Books, 2003).
Marx, K. and Engels, F., *Selected Correspondence* (Moscow, Progress, 1955).
-------------------------- *Articles on Britain* (London: Lawrence & Wishart Ltd 1971).
------------------------- *The Communist Manifesto* (London, Verso, 1998).
Mason, T. W., 'Nineteenth-Century Cromwell', *Past and Present*, No.40 (July 1968).
McElligott, J., 'William Hone (1780-1842), Print Culture and the Nature of Radicalism' in A Hessayon and D Finnegan (eds.), *Varieties of Seventeenth- and Early Eighteenth-Century Radicalism in Context* (Farnham, Ashgate, 2011), pp.241-61.
Mendle, M. (ed), *The Putney Debates of 1647* (Cambridge, CUP, 2001).
Merriman, R. B., *Six Contemporaneous Revolutions* (Oxford, Clarendon Press, 1938).
Moote, Lloyd A., 'The Preconditions of Revolution' in G. Parker and L. M. Smith, *The General Crisis of the Seventeenth Century* (London, Routledge, Kegan, Paul, 1978).
Morgan, D. W., 'The Father of Revisionism Revisited', *Journal of Modern History* 51 (1979).
Morrill, J., *The Revolt of the Provinces* (London, Longman, 1976).

---------- 'Provincial Squires and "Middling Sorts" in the Great Rebellion', *The Historical Journal*, Vol. 20, No. 1 (Mar. 1977), pp.229-36.
---------- *The Nature of the English Revolution* (London, Longman, 1993).
---------- 'Conflict Probable or Inevitable?', *New Left Review* 207 (Sept.-Oct. 1994), pp.113-23.
---------- 'Revisionism's Wounded Legacies', *Huntington Library Quarterly*, Vol. 78, No. 4 (Winter 2015), pp.577-594.
Morrill, John and Baker, Phillip, 'The Case of the Armie Truly Re-stated' in M Mendle (ed.), *The Putney Debates of 1647, the army the levellers and the English state*, pp.103-24
Morton, A. L., *The World of the Ranters* (London, Lawrence and Wishart, 1970).
---------------- *Freedom in Arms, A Selection of Leveller Writings* (London, Lawrence and Wishart, 1974).
Mousnier, R., 'The Fronde', in R. Forster and J. P. Greene, *Preconditions of Revolution in Early Modern Europe.*
Norris, C., *Uncritical Theory* (London, Lawrence and Wishart, 1992).
O'Brien, M., 'Postmodernism and British History' in J. Rees (ed.), *Essays on Historical Materialism.*
Parker, D. (ed.), *Ideology, Absolutism and the English Revolution, debates of the British Communist Historians* (London, Lawrence and Wishart, 2008).
Parker, G. and Smith L. M. (eds.), *The General Crisis of the Seventeenth Century* (London, Routledge, Kegan, Paul, 1978).
Parker, G., 'Crisis and Catastrophe: The Global Crisis of the Seventeenth Century Reconsidered', *The American Historical Review*, Vol.113, No.4 (Oct. 2008).
Peacey, J., 'The People of the Agreements: the Levellers, Civil War Radicalism and Political Participation' in P. Baker and E. Vernon, (eds), *The Agreements of the People, the Levellers and the constitutional crisis of the English revolution.* (Basingstoke, Palgrave Macmillan, 2012), pp.76-96.
----------- 'The hunting of the Leveller: the sophistication of parliamentarian propaganda, 1647–53', *Historical Research* 78, No.199 (February 2005)
----------- 'John Lilburne and the Long Parliament', *The Historical Journal* 43, No.3 (Sep. 2000).
Peacock, E., 'Notes on the Life of Thomas Rainsbourgh', *Archaeologia* 46 (1880).
Pease, T. C., *The Leveller Movement* (Gloucester, Mass., Peter Smith, 1965).
-------------- review, *The American Historical Review* 50, No.2 (Jan. 1945), pp.315-16.
Petegorsky, D., *Left Wing Democracy in the English Civil War* (London, Gollancz, 1940).
Raymond, J. and Moxham, N., *News Networks in Early Modern Europe* (Leiden, Brill, 2016).
Rees, J., 'The rising bourgeoisie', *International Socialism*, No.46 (London, Spring 1990), pp.159-165.
--------- 'Revolution Denied' in L. German and R. Hoveman (eds.) *A Socialist*

Review (London, Bookmarks, 1998).
--------- *The Algebra of Revolution* (London, Routledge, 1998).
--------- (ed.), *Essays on Historical Materialism* (London, Bookmarks, 1998).
--------- *The Leveller Revolution* (London, Verso, 2016).
--------- (ed.), *John Lilburne and the Levellers* (London, Routledge, 2018).
--------- 'The Levellers, the Labouring Classes, and the Poor', *Bunyan Studies*, No.24 (2020).
--------- *The Fiery Spirits* (London, Verso, forthcoming 2025).
Richardson, R. C., *The Debate on the English Revolution* (London, Methuen, 1977).
Robertson, G., *The Tyrannicide Brief, The Story of the Man who sent Charles I to the Scaffold* (London, Chatto and Windus, 2005).
Russell, C., *The Causes of the English Civil War* (Oxford, OUP, 1990).
Samuel, R., 'British Marxist Historians, 1880–1980: Part One', *New Left Review* 120 (1980).
Schenk, W., *The Concern for Social Justice in the Puritan Revolution* (London, Longmans, 1948).
Sharpe, A. (ed.), *The English Levellers* (Cambridge, CUP, 1998).
Sharpe, B., 'The Place of the People in the English Revolution', *Theory and Society*, Vol.14, No.1 (Jan. 1985).
Sharpe, K., *The Personal Rule of Charles I* (New Haven, Yale, 1996).
Shaw, H., *The Levellers* (London, Longman, 1968).
Southern, A., *Forlorn Hope, Soldier Radicals of the Seventeenth Century* (Lewes, The Book Guild, 2001).
Stevenson, J. and Cook, C., *The Slump, Society and Politics during the Depression* (London, Quartet, 1977).
Stiles, E., *A History of Three Judges of Charles I* (Hartford, Conn., 1794).
Stone, L., 'The English Revolution' in in R. Forster and J. P. Greene, *Preconditions of Revolution in Early Modern Europe* (Baltimore, John Hopkins Press, 1970).
Sturza, M., *The London Revolution 1640-1643* (New York, Mad Duck, 2022).
Taft, B., 'The Council of Officers' Agreement of the People, 1648/9', *The Historical Journal*, Vol.28, No.1 (Mar. 1985), pp.169-85.
Taylor, S. and Tapsell G. (eds.), *The Nature of the English Revolution Revisited* (Woodbridge, Boydell and Brewer, 2013).
Thomas, K., 'The Levellers and the Franchise' in G E Aylmer, (ed.) *The Interregnum, the Quest for a Settlement* (Basingstoke, MacMillan, 1972), pp.57-79.
Thompson, C., 'Maximilian Petty and the Putney Debate on the Franchise', *Past and Present*, No.88 (Aug. 1980), pp.63-9.
Thompson, E. P., *The Poverty of Theory and Other Essays* (London, Merlin, 1978).
Tolmie, M., *The Triumph of the Saints, the Separate Churches of London 1616-1649* (Cambridge, CUP, 1977).

Trevor-Roper, H. R., 'The General Crisis of the Seventeenth Century', T. H. Aston (ed.), *Crisis in Europe 1560-1660* (London, RKP, 1965).
Trotsky, L., 'Where is Britain Going?' in L. Trotsky, *Trotsky's Writings on Britain*, Vol.2 (London, New Park, 1974), pp.85-93.
------------ *Trotsky's Writings on Britain*, Vol.2 (London, New Park, 1974).
Tyacke, N., ed. *The English Revolution c.1590-1720, Politics, Religion and Communities* (Manchester, MUP, 2007).
Vallance, E., 'Reborn John? The Eighteenth-century Afterlife of John Lilburne', in *History Workshop Journal*, No.74 (Autumn, 2012).
Vernon, E. and Baker, P., 'Appendix I, *Les principes, fondement et gouverement d'une republique*: The French *Agreement of the People*', in E. Vernon and P. Baker, *The Agreements of the People, The Levellers, and the Constitutional Crisis of the English Revolution* (London, Palgrave Macmillan, 2012).
Villari, R., *The Revolt of Naples* (Oxford, Polity, 1993).
Walter, J., 'Kissing Cousins? Social History/Political History before and after the Revisionist Moment', *Huntington Library Quarterly* 78, No.4 (Winter 2015).
Westrich, S. A., *The Ormee of Bordeaux, A Revolution during the Fronde* (Baltimore, John Hopkins University Press, 1972).
Wickham, C. *Marxist History-writing for the Twenty-first Century* (Oxford, OUP, 2007)
Williamson, H. R., *Four Stuart Portraits* (London, Evans Brothers, 1949).
Wintringham. *Mutiny. Mutinies from Spartacus to Invergordon* (London, Stanley Nott, 1936).
Wolfe, D., *Leveller Manifestoes of the Puritan Revolution* (Frank Cass 1967).
Wood, E. Meiksins, 'The Separation of the Economic and the Political in Capitalism', *New Left Review*, 127 (May-June 1981).
---------------------- *The Pristine Culture of Capitalism* (London, Verso, 1991).
---------------------- *The Origin of Capitalism* (London, Verso, 2016).
---------------------- *The Pristine Culture of Capitalism* (London, Verso, 2015).
Wood, E. Meiksins and Wood N., *The Trumpet of Sedition, Political Theory and the Rise of Capitalism 1509-1688* (London, Pluto Press, 1997).
Woolrych, A., 'Preface to the 1992 Edition' in W Clarke, *The Clarke Papers* (edited and introduced by C. H. Firth, London, Royal Historical Society, 1992).
---------------- *Soldiers and Statesmen, The General Council of the Army and its Debates* (Oxford, OUP, 1987).
Worden, B., 'The Levellers in history and memory, c.1660-1960' in M Mendle (ed.), *The Putney Debates of 1647, the army the levellers and the English state* (Cambridge, CUP, 2001).
-------------- *Roundhead Reputations* (London, Penguin, 2001).
Yerby, G., *The Economic Causes of the English Civil War* (London, Routledge, 2020).
Zinn, H., A People's History of the United States (London, Longman, 1980).

Index